SEA WARFARE

SEA WARFARE

by

Rudyard Kipling

UNIFORM
PRESS

Uniform Press Ltd
66 Charlotte Street
London
W1T 4QE

www.uniformpress.co.uk

Fringes of the Fleet first published in 1915
Tales of 'The Trade' first published in 1916
Destroyers at Jutland first published in 1916
This edition published in 2015 by Uniform Press Ltd

978-1-910500-132

5 4 3 2 1

Printed in India by Imprint Digital
Cover Design by Lucy Duckworth
Insides by Charlotte Glyde

CONTENTS

˙The Fringes of the Fleet

1915

In Lowestoft a boat was laid,
    Mark well what I do say!
And she was built for the herring trade,
    But she has gone a-rovin', a-rovin', a-rovin',
    The Lord knows where!

They gave her Government coal to burn,
And a Q.F. gun at bow and stern,
And sent her out a-rovin', etc.

Her skipper was mate of a bucko ship
Which always killed one man per trip,
So he is used to rovin', etc.

8

Her mate was skipper of a chapel in Wales,
And so he fights in topper and tails –
Religi-ous tho' rovin', etc.

Her engineer is fifty-eight,
So he's prepared to meet his fate,
Which ain't unlikely rovin', etc.

Her leading-stoker's seventeen,
So he don't know what the Judgments mean,
Unless he cops 'em rovin', etc.

Her cook was chef in the Lost Dogs' Home,
  Mark well what I do say!
And I'm sorry for Fritz when they all come
  A-rovin', a-rovin', a-roarin' and a-rovin',
  Round the North Sea rovin',
  The Lord knows where!

THE AUXILIARIES

I

THE Navy is very old and very wise. Much of her wisdom is on record and available for reference; but more of it works in the unconscious blood of those who serve her. She has a thousand years of experience, and can find precedent or parallel for any situation that the force of the weather or the malice of the King's enemies may bring about.

The main principles of sea-warfare hold good throughout all ages, and, *so far as the Navy has been allowed to put out her strength,* these principles have been applied over all the seas of the world. For matters of detail the Navy, to whom all days are alike, has simply returned to the practice and resurrected the spirit of old days.

In the late French wars, a merchant sailing out of a Channel port might in a few hours find himself laid by the heels and under way for a French prison. His Majesty's ships of the Line, and even the big frigates, took little part in policing the waters for him, unless he were in convoy. The sloops, cutters, gun-brigs, and local craft of all kinds were supposed to look after that, while the Line was busy elsewhere. So the merchants passed resolutions against the inadequate protection afforded to the trade, and the narrow seas were full of single-ship actions; mail-packets, West Country brigs, and fat East Indiamen fighting, for their own hulls and cargo, anything that the watchful French ports sent against them; the sloops and cutters bearing a hand if they happened to be within reach.

THE OLDEST NAVY

It was a brutal age, ministered to by hard-fisted men, and we had put it a hundred decent years behind us when - it all comes back again! Today there are no prisons for the crews of merchantmen, but they can go to the bottom by mine and torpedo even more quickly than their ancestors were run into Le Havre. The submarine takes the place of the privateer; the Line, as in the old wars, is occupied, bombarding and blockading, elsewhere, but the sea-borne traffic must continue, and that is being looked after by the lineal descendants of the crews of the long extinct cutters and sloops and gun-brigs. The hour struck, and they reappeared, to the tune of fifty thousand odd men in more than two thousand ships, of which I have seen a few hundred. Words of command may have changed a little, the tools are certainly more complex, but the spirit of the new crews who come to the old job is utterly unchanged. It is the same fierce, hard-living, heavy-handed, very cunning service out of which the Navy as we know it today was born. It is called indifferently the Trawler and Auxiliary Fleet. It is chiefly composed of fishermen, but it takes in every one who may have maritime tastes – from retired admirals to the sons of the sea-cook. It exists for the benefit of the traffic and the annoyance of the enemy. Its doings are recorded by flags stuck into charts; its casualties are buried in obscure corners of the newspapers. The Grand Fleet knows it slightly; the restless light cruisers who chaperon it from the background are more intimate; the destroyers working off unlighted coasts over unmarked shoals come, as you might say, in direct contact with it; the submarine alternately praises and – since one periscope is very like another – curses its activities; but the steady procession of traffic in home waters, liner and tramp, six every sixty minutes, blesses it altogether.

Since this most Christian war includes laying mines in the fairways of traffic, and since these mines may be laid at any time by German submarines especially built for the work, or by neutral ships, all fairways must be swept continuously day and night. When a nest of mines is reported, traffic must be hung up or deviated till it is cleared out. When traffic comes up Channel it must be examined for contraband and other things; and the examining tugs lie out in a blaze of lights to remind ships of this. Months ago, when the war was young, the tugs did not know what to look for specially. Now they do. All this mine searching and reporting and sweeping, *plus* the direction and examination of the traffic, *plus* the laying of our own ever-shifting mine-fields, is part of the Trawler Fleet's

12

work, because the Navy-as-we-knew-it is busy elsewhere. And there is always the enemy submarine with a price on her head, whom the Trawler Fleet hunts and traps with zeal and joy. Add to this, that there are boats, fishing for real fish, to be protected in their work at sea or chased off dangerous areas whither, because they are strictly forbidden to go, they naturally repair, and you will begin to get some idea of what the Trawler and Auxiliary Fleet does.

The Ships and the Men

Now, imagine the acreage of several dock-basins crammed, gunwale to gunwale, with brown and umber and ochre and rust-red steam-trawlers, tugs, harbour-boats, and yachts once clean and respectable, now dirty and happy. Throw in fish-steamers, surprise-packets of unknown lines and indescribable junks, sampans, lorchas, catamarans, and General Service stink-pontoons filled with indescribable apparatus, manned by men no dozen of whom seem to talk the same dialect or wear the same clothes. The mustard-coloured jersey who is cleaning a six-pounder on a Hull boat clips his words between his teeth and would be happier in Gaelic. The whitish singlet and grey trousers held up by what is obviously his soldier brother's spare regimental belt is pure Lowestoft. The complete blue-serge-and-soot suit passing a wire down a hatch is Glasgow as far as you can hear him, which is a fair distance, because he wants something done to the other end of the wire, and the flat-faced boy who should be attending to it hails from the remoter Hebrides, and is looking at a girl on the dock-edge. The bow-legged man in the ulster and green-worsted comforter is a warm Grimsby skipper, worth several thousands. He and his crew, who are mostly his own relations, keep themselves to themselves, and save their money. The pirate with the red beard, barking over the rail at a friend with gold earrings, comes from Skye. The friend is West Country. The noticeably insignificant man with the soft and deprecating eye is skipper and part-owner of the big slashing Iceland trawler on which he droops like a flower. She is built to almost Western Ocean lines, carries a little boat-deck aft with tremendous stanchions, has a nose cocked high against ice and sweeping seas, and resembles a hawk-moth at rest. The small, sniffing man is reported to be a 'holy terror at sea.'

Hunters And Fishers

The child in the Pullman-car uniform just going ashore is a wireless operator, aged nineteen. He is attached to a flagship at least 120 feet long, under an admiral aged twenty-five, who was, till the other day, third mate of a North Atlantic tramp, but who now leads a squadron of six trawlers to hunt submarines. The principle is simple enough. Its application depends on circumstances and surroundings. One class of German submarines meant for murder off the coasts may use a winding and rabbit-like track between shoals where the

14

choice of water is limited. Their career is rarely long, but, while it lasts, moderately exciting. Others, told off for deep-sea assassinations, are attended to quite quietly and without any excitement at all. Others, again, work the inside of the North Sea, making no distinction between neutrals and Allied ships. These carry guns, and since their work keeps them a good deal on the surface, the Trawler Fleet, as we know, engages them there – the submarine firing, sinking, and rising again in unexpected quarters; the trawler firing, dodging, and trying to ram. The trawlers are strongly built, and can stand a great deal of punishment. Yet again, other German submarines hang about the skirts of fishing-fleets and fire into the brown of them. When the war was young this gave splendidly 'frightful' results, but for some reason or other the game is not as popular as it used to be.

Lastly, there are German submarines who perish by ways so curious and inexplicable that one could almost credit the whispered idea (it must come from the Scotch skippers) that the ghosts of the women they drowned pilot them to destruction. But what form these shadows take – whether of 'The Lusitania Ladies,' or humbler stewardesses and hospital nurses – and what lights or sounds the thing fancies it sees or hears before it is blotted out, no man will ever know. The main fact is that the work is being done. Whether it was necessary or politic to re-awaken by violence every sporting instinct of a sea-going people is a question which the enemy may have to consider later on.

*D*AWN *off the Foreland – the young flood making*
     Jumbled and short and steep –
Black in the hollows and bright where it's breaking –
     Awkward water to sweep.
     'Mines reported in the fairway,
     Warn all traffic and detain.
''Sent up Unity, Claribel, Assyrian, Stormcock, and Golden Gain.'

Noon off the Foreland--the first ebb making
     Lumpy and strong in the bight.
Boom after boom, and the golf-hut shaking
     And the jackdaws wild with fright!
     'Mines located in the fairway,
     Boats now working up the chain,
'Sweepers – Unity, Claribel, Assyrian,
     Stormcock and Golden Gain.'

Dusk off the Foreland – the last light going
  And the traffic crowding through,
And five damned trawlers with their syreens blowing
  Heading the whole review!
  'Sweep completed in the fairway.
  'No more mines remain.
  ''Sent back Unity, Claribel, Assyrian, Stormcock, and
Golden Gain.'

THE AUXILIARIES

II

THE Trawlers seem to look on mines as more or less fairplay. But with the torpedo it is otherwise. A Yarmouth man lay on his hatch, his gear neatly stowed away below, and told me that another Yarmouth boat had 'gone up,' with all hands except one. ''Twas a submarine. Not a mine,' said he. 'They never gave our boys no chance. Na! She was a Yarmouth boat – we knew 'em all. They never gave the boys no chance.' He was a submarine hunter, and he illustrated by means of matches placed at various angles how the blindfold business is conducted. 'And then,' he ended, 'there's always what *he'll* do. You've got to think that out for yourself – while you're working above him – same as if 'twas fish.' I should not care to be hunted for the life in shallow waters by a man who knows every bank and pothole of them, even if I had not killed his friends the week before. Being nearly all fishermen they discuss their work in terms of fish, and put in their leisure fishing overside, when they sometimes pull up ghastly souvenirs. But they all want guns. Those who have three-pounders clamour for sixes; sixes for twelves; and the twelve-pound aristocracy dream of four-inchers on anti-aircraft mountings for the benefit of roving Zeppelins. They will all get them in time, and I fancy it will be long ere they give them up. One West Country mate announced that 'a gun is a handy thing to have aboard – always.' 'But in peacetime?' I said. 'Wouldn't it be in the way?'

'We'm used to 'em now,' was the smiling answer. 'Niver go to sea again without a gun – I wouldn't – if I had my way. It keeps all hands pleased-like.'

They talk about men in the Army who will never willingly go back to civil life. What of the fishermen who have tasted something sharper than salt water - and what of the young third and fourth mates who have held independent commands for nine months past? One of them said to me quite irrelevantly: 'I used to be the animal that got up the trunks for the women on baggage-days in the old Bodiam Castle,' and he mimicked their requests for 'the large brown box,' or 'the black dress basket,' as a freed soul might scoff at his old life in the flesh.

'A COMMON SWEEPER'

My sponsor and chaperon in this Elizabethan world of eighteenth-century seamen was an A.B. who had gone down in the Landrail, assisted at the Heligoland fight, seen the Blücher sink and the bombs dropped on our boats when we tried to save the drowning ('Whereby,' as he said, 'those

Germans died gottstrafin' their own country because we didn't wait to be strafed'), and has now found more peaceful days in an Office ashore. He led me across many decks from craft to craft to study the various appliances that they specialise in. Almost our last was what a North Country trawler called a 'common sweeper,' that is to say, a mine-sweeper. She was at tea in her shirt-sleeves, and she protested loudly that there was 'nothing in sweeping.' "See that wire rope?' she said. 'Well, it leads through that lead to the ship which you're sweepin' with. She makes her end fast and you make yourn. Then you sweep together at whichever depth you've agreed upon between you, by means of that arrangement there which regulates the depth. They give you a glass sort o' thing for keepin' your distance from the other ship, but that's not wanted if you know each other. Well, then, you sweep, as the sayin' is. There's nothin' in it. You sweep till this wire rope fouls the bloomin' mines. Then you go on till they appear on the surface, so to say, and then you explodes them by means of shootin' at 'em with that rifle in the galley there. There's nothin' in sweepin' more than that.'

'And if you hit a mine?' I asked.

'You go up – but you hadn't ought to hit em', if you're careful. The thing is to get hold of the first mine all right, and then you go on to the next, and so on, in a way o' speakin'.'

'And you can fish, too, 'tween times,' said a voice from the next boat. A man leaned over and returned a borrowed mug. They talked about fishing – notably that once they caught some red mullet, which the 'common sweeper' and his neighbour both agreed was 'not natural in those waters.' As for mere sweeping, it bored them profoundly to talk about it. I only learned later as part of the natural history of mines, that if you rake the tri-nitro-toluol by hand out of a German mine you develop eruptions and skin-poisoning. But on the authority of two experts, there is nothing in sweeping. Nothing whatever!

A Block in the Traffic

Now imagine, not a pistol-shot from these crowded quays, a little Office hung round with charts that are pencilled and noted over various shoals and soundings. There is a movable list of the boats at work, with quaint and domestic names. Outside the window lies the packed harbor – outside that again the line of traffic up and down – a stately cinema-show of six ships to the hour. For the moment the film sticks. A boat – probably a 'common sweeper' – reports an obstruction in a traffic lane a few miles away. She has found and exploded one mine. The Office heard the dull boom of it before the wireless report came in. In all likelihood there is a nest of them there. It is possible that a submarine may have got in last night between certain shoals and laid them out. The shoals are being shepherded in case she is hidden anywhere, but the boundaries of the newly discovered mine-area must be fixed and the traffic deviated. There is a tramp outside with tugs in attendance. She has hit something and is leaking badly. Where shall she go? The Office gives her her destination - the harbour is too full for her to settle down here. She swings off between

21

the faithful tugs. Down coast some one asks by wireless if they shall hold up their traffic. It is exactly like a signaller 'offering' a train to the next block. 'Yes,' the Office replies. 'Wait a while. If it's what we think, there will be a little delay. If it isn't what we think, there will be a little longer delay.' Meantime, sweepers are nosing round the suspected area – 'looking for cuckoos' eggs,' as a voice suggests; and a patrol-boat lathers her way down coast to catch and stop anything that may be on the move, for skippers are sometimes rather careless. Words begin to drop out of the air into the chart-hung Office. 'Six and a half cables south, fifteen east' of something or other. 'Mark it well, and tell them to work up from there,' is the order. 'Another mine exploded!' 'Yes, and we heard that too,' says the Office. 'What about the submarine?' *'Elizabeth Huggins* reports…'

Elizabeth's scandal must be fairly high flavoured, for a torpedo-boat of immoral aspect slings herself out of harbour and hastens to share it. If Elizabeth has not spoken the truth, there may be words between the parties. For the present a penciled suggestion seems to cover the case, together with a demand, as far as one can make out, for 'more common sweepers.' They will be forthcoming very shortly. Those at work have got the run of the mines now, and are busily howking them up. A trawler-skipper wishes to speak to the Office. 'They' have ordered him out, but his boiler, most of it, is on the quay at the present time, and 'ye'll remember, it's the same wi' my foremast an' port rigging, sir.' The Office does not precisely remember, but if boiler and foremast are on the quay the rest of the ship had better stay alongside. The skipper falls away relieved. (He scraped a tramp a few nights ago in a bit of a sea.) There is a little mutter of gun-fire somewhere across the grey water where a fleet is at work. A monitor as broad as she is long comes back from wherever the trouble is, slips through the harbour mouth, all wreathed with signals, is received by two motherly lighters, and, to all appearance, goes to sleep between them. The Office does not even look up; for that is not in their department. They have found a trawler to replace the boilerless one. Her name is slid into the rack. The immoral torpedo-boat flounces back to her moorings. Evidently what Elizabeth Huggins said was not evidence. The messages and replies begin again as the day closes.

The Night Patrol

Return now to the inner harbour. At twilight there was a stir among the packed craft like the separation of dried tea-leaves in water. The swing-bridge across the basin shut against us. A boat shot out of the jam, took the narrow exit at a fair seven knots and rounded in the outer harbour with all the pomp of a flagship, which was exactly what she was. Others followed, breaking away from every quarter in silence. Boat after boat fell into line – gear stowed away, spars and buoys in order on their clean decks, guns cast loose and ready, wheel-house windows darkened, and everything in order for a day or a week or a month out. There was no word anywhere. The interrupted foot-traffic stared at them as they slid past below. A woman beside me waved her hand to a man on one of them, and I saw his face light as he waved back. The boat where they had demonstrated for me with matches was the last. Her skipper hadn't thought it worth while to tell me that he was going that evening. Then the line straightened up and stood out to sea.

'You never said this was going to happen,' I said reproachfully to my A.B.

'No more I did,' said he. 'It's the night-patrol going out. Fact is, I'm so used to the bloomin' evolution that it never struck me to mention it as you might say.'

Next morning I was at service in a man-of-war, and even as we came to the prayer that the Navy might 'be a safeguard to such as pass upon the sea on their lawful occasions,' I saw the long procession of traffic resuming up and down the Channel – six ships to the hour. It has been hung up for a bit, they said.

FAREWELL and adieu to you, Greenwich
          ladies,
Farewell and adieu to you, ladies ashore!
For we've received orders to work to the
          eastward
Where we hope in a short time to strafe 'em
          some more.

We'll duck and we'll dive like little tin turtles,
We'll duck and we'll dive underneath the
          North Seas,
Until we strike something that doesn't
          expect us,
From here to Cuxhaven it's go as you please!
The first thing we did was to dock in a
          mine-field,
Which isn't a place where repairs should be
          done;

And there we lay doggo in twelve-fathom
        water
With tri-nitro-toluol hogging our run.

The next thing we did, we rose under a
        Zeppelin,
With his shiny big belly half blocking the
        sky.
But what in the — Heavens can you do with
        six-pounders?
So we fired what we had and we bade him
        good-bye.

SUBMARINES

I

THE chief business of the Trawler Fleet is to attend to the traffic. The submarine in her sphere attends to the enemy. Like the destroyer, the submarine has created its own type of officer and man – with language and traditions apart from the rest of the Service, and yet at heart unchangingly of the Service. Their business is to run monstrous risks from earth, air, and water, in what, to be of any use, must be the coldest of cold blood.

The commander's is more a one-man job, as the crew's is more team-work, than any other employment afloat. That is why the relations between submarine officers and men are what they are. They play hourly for each other's lives with Death the Umpire always at their elbow on tiptoe to give them 'out.'

There is a stretch of water, once dear to amateur yachtsmen, now given over to scouts, submarines, destroyers, and, of course, contingents of trawlers. We were waiting the return

27

of some boats which were due to report. A couple surged up the still harbour in the afternoon light and tied up beside their sisters. There climbed out of them three or four high-booted, sunken-eyed pirates clad in sweaters, under jackets that a stoker of the last generation would have disowned. This was their first chance to compare notes at close hand. Together they lamented the loss of a Zeppelin – 'a perfect mug of a Zepp,' who had come down very low and offered one of them a sitting shot. 'But what can you do with our guns? I gave him what I had, and then he started bombing.'

'I know he did,' another said. 'I heard him. That's what brought me down to you. I thought he had you that last time.'

'No, I was forty foot under when he hove out the big-un. What happened to you?'

'My steering-gear jammed just after I went down, and I had to go round in circles till I got it straightened out. But wasn't he a mug!'

'Was he the brute with the patch on his port side?' a sister-boat demanded.

'No! This fellow had just been hatched. He was almost sitting on the water, heaving bombs over.'

'And my blasted steering-gear went and chose then to go wrong,' the other commander mourned. 'I thought his last little egg was going to get me!'

Half an hour later, I was formally introduced to three or four quite strange, quite immaculate officers, freshly shaved, and a little tired about the eyes, whom I thought I had met before.

Meantime (it was on the hour of evening drinks) one of the boats was still unaccounted for. No one talked of her. They rather discussed motor-cars and Admiralty constructors, but – it felt like that queer twilight watch at the front when the homing aeroplanes drop in. Presently a signaller entered. 'V 42 outside, sir; wants to know which channel she shall use.' 'Oh, thank you. Tell her to take so-and so.'… Mine, remember, was vermouth and bitters, and later on V 42 himself found a soft chair and joined the committee of instruction. Those next for duty, as well as those in training, wished to hear what was going on, and who had shifted what to where, and how certain arrangements had worked. They were told in language not to be found in any printable book. Questions and answers were alike Hebrew to one listener, but he gathered that every boat carried a second in command – a strong, persevering youth, who seemed responsible for everything that went wrong, from a motor cylinder to a torpedo. Then somebody touched on the mercantile marine and its habits.

Said one philosopher: 'They can't be expected to take any more risks than they do. I wouldn't, if I was a skipper. I'd loose off at any blessed periscope I saw.'

'That's all very fine. You wait till you've had a patriotic tramp trying to strafe you at your own back-door,' said another.

Some one told a tale of a man with a voice, notable even in a Service where men are not trained to whisper. He was coming back, empty-handed, dirty, tired, and best left alone.

From the peace of the German side he had entered our hectic home-waters, where the usual tramp shelled, and by miraculous luck, crumpled his periscope. Another man might have dived, but Boanerges kept on rising. Majestic and wrathful he rose personally through his main hatch, and at 2000 yards (have I said it was a still day?) addressed the tramp. Even at that distance she gathered it was a Naval officer with a grievance, and by the time he ran alongside she was in a state of coma, but managed to stammer: 'Well, sir, at least you'll admit that our shooting was pretty good.'

'And that,' said my informant, 'put the lid on!' Boanerges went down lest he should be tempted to murder; and the tramp affirms she heard him rumbling beneath her, like an inverted thunder-storm, for fifteen minutes.

'All those tramps ought to be disarmed, and we ought to have all their guns,' said a voice out of a corner.

'What? Still worrying over your 'mug'?' some one replied.

'He was a mug!' went on the man of one idea. 'If I'd had a couple of twelves even, I could have strafed him proper. I don't know whether I shall mutiny, or desert, or write to the First Sea Lord about it.'

'Strafe all Admiralty constructors to begin with. I could build a better boat with a 4-inch lathe and a sardine-tin than ----,' the speaker named her by letter and number.

'That's pure jealousy,' her commander explained to the company. 'Ever since I installed – ahem! – my patent electric washbasin he's been intriguin' to get her. Why? We know he doesn't wash. He'd only use the basin to keep beer in.'

However often one meets it, as in this war one meets it at every turn, one never gets used to the Holy Spirit of Man at his job. The 'common sweeper,' growling over his mug of tea that there was 'nothing in sweepin',' and these idly chaffing men, new shaved and attired, from the gates of Death which had let them through for the fiftieth time, were all of the same fabric - incomprehensible, I should imagine, to the enemy. And the stuff held good throughout all the world – from the Dardanelles to the Baltic, where only a little while ago another batch of submarines had slipped in and begun to be busy. I had spent some of the afternoon in looking through reports of submarine work in the Sea of Marmora. They read like the diary of energetic weasels in an overcrowded chicken-run, and the results for each boat were tabulated something like a cricket score. There were no maiden overs. One came across jewels of price set in the flat official phraseology. For example, one man who was describing some steps he was taking to remedy certain defects, interjected casually: 'At this point I had to go under for a little, as a man in a boat was trying to grab my periscope with his hand.' No reference before or after to the said man or his fate. Again: 'Came across a dhow with a Turkish skipper. He seemed so miserable that I let him go.' And elsewhere in those waters, a submarine overhauled a steamer full of Turkish passengers, some of whom, arguing on their allies' lines, promptly leaped overboard. Our boat fished them out and returned them, for she was not killing civilians.

In another affair, which included several ships (now at the bottom) and one submarine, the commander relaxes enough to note that:

'The men behaved very well under direct and flanking fire from rifles at about fifteen yards.' This was not, I believe, the submarine that fought the Turkish cavalry on the beach. And in addition to matters much more marvellous than any I have hinted at, the reports deal with repairs and shifts and contrivances carried through in the face of dangers that read like the last delirium of romance. One boat went down the Straits and found herself rather canted over to one side. A mine and chain had jammed under her forward diving-plane. So far as I made out, she shook it off by standing on her head and jerking backwards; or it may have been, for the thing has occurred more than once, she merely rose as much as she could, when she could, and then 'released it by hand,' as the official phrase goes.

Four Nightmares

And who, a few months ago, could have invented, or having invented, would have dared to print such a nightmare as this: There was a boat in the North Sea who ran into a net and was caught by the nose. She rose, still entangled, meaning to cut the thing away on the surface. But a Zeppelin in waiting saw and bombed her, and she had to go down again at once - but not too wildly or she would get herself more wrapped up than ever. She went down, and by slow working and weaving and wriggling, guided only by guesses at the meaning of each scrape and grind of the net on her blind forehead, at last she drew clear. Then she sat on the bottom and thought. The question was whether she should go back at once and warn her confederates against the trap, or wait till the destroyers which she knew the Zeppelin would have signalled for, should come out to finish her still entangled, as they would suppose, in the net? It was a simple calculation of comparative speeds and positions, and when it was worked out she decided to try for the double event. Within a few minutes of the time she had allowed for them, she heard the twitter of four destroyers' screws quartering above her; rose; got her shot in; saw one destroyer crumple; hung round till another took the wreck in tow; said good-bye to the spare brace (she was at the end of her supplies), and reached the rendezvous in time to turn her friends.

And since we are dealing in nightmares, here are two more – one genuine, the other, mercifully, false. There was a boat not only at, but in the mouth of a river--well home in German territory. She was spotted, and went under, her commander perfectly aware that there was not more than five feet of water over her conning-tower, so that even a torpedo-boat, let alone a destroyer, would hit it if she came over.

But nothing hit anything. The search was conducted on scientific principles while they sat on the silt and suffered. Then the commander heard the rasp of a wire trawl sweeping over his hull. It was not a nice sound, but there happened to be a couple of gramophones aboard, and he turned them both on to drown it. And in due time that boat got home with everybody's hair of just the same colour as when they had started!

The other nightmare arose out of silence and imagination. A boat had gone to bed on the bottom in a spot where she might reasonably expect to be looked for, but it was a convenient jumping-off, or up, place for the work in hand. About the bad hour of 2.30 A.M. the commander was waked by one of his men, who whispered to him: 'They've got the chains on us, sir!' Whether it was pure nightmare, an hallucination of long wakefulness, something relaxing and releasing in that packed box of machinery, or the disgustful reality, the commander could not tell, but it had all the makings of panic in it. So the Lord and long training put it into his head to reply! 'Have they? Well, we shan't be coming up till nine o'clock this morning. We'll see about it then. Turn out that light, please.'

He did not sleep, but the dreamer and the others did, morning came and he gave the order to rise, and she rose unhampered, and he saw the grey, smeared seas from above once again, he said it was a very refreshing sight.

Lastly, which is on all fours with the gamble of the chase, a man was coming home rather bored after an uneventful trip. It was necessary for him to sit on the bottom for awhile, and there he played patience.

Of a sudden it struck him, as a vow and an omen, that if he worked out the next game correctly he would go up and strafe something. The cards fell all in order. He went up at once and found himself alongside a German, whom, as he had promised and prophesied to himself, he destroyed. She was a mine-layer, and needed only a jar to dissipate like a cracked electric-light bulb. He was somewhat impressed by the contrast between the single-handed game fifty feet below, the ascent, the attack, the amazing result, and when he descended again, his cards just as he had left them.

The ships destroy us above
　　　And ensnare us beneath.
We arise, we lie down, and we move
　　　In the belly of Death.

The ships have a thousand eyes
　　　To mark where we come…
And the mirth of a seaport dies
　　　When our blow gets home.

SUBMARINES

II

I was honoured by a glimpse into this veiled life in a boat which was merely practising between trips. Submarines are like cats. They never tell 'who they were with last night,' and they sleep as much as they can. If you board a submarine off duty you generally see a perspective of fore-shortened fattish men laid all along. The men say that except at certain times it is rather an easy life, with relaxed regulations about smoking, calculated to make a man put on flesh. One requires well-padded nerves. Many of the men do not appear on deck throughout the whole trip. After all, why should they if they don't want to? They know that they are responsible in their department for their comrades' lives as their comrades are responsible for theirs. What's the use of flapping about? Better lay in some magazines and cigarettes.

When we set forth there had been some trouble in the fairway, and a mined neutral, whose misfortune all bore with exemplary calm, was careened on a near-by shoal.

37

'Suppose there are more mines knocking about?' I suggested.

'We'll hope there aren't,' was the soothing reply. 'Mines are all Joss. You either hit 'em or you don't. And if you do, they don't always go off. They scrape alongside.'

'What's the etiquette then?'

'Shut off both propellers and hope.'

We were dodging various craft down the harbour when a squadron of trawlers came out on our beam, at that extravagant rate of speed which unlimited Government coal always leads to. They were led by an ugly, upstanding, black-sided buccaneer with twelve-pounders.

'Ah! That's the King of the Trawlers. Isn't he carrying dog, too! Give him room!' one said.

We were all in the narrowed harbour mouth together.

"There's my youngest daughter. Take a look at her!" some one hummed as a punctilious navy cap slid by on a very near bridge.

'We'll fall in behind him. They're going over to the neutral. Then they'll sweep. By the bye, did you hear about one of the passengers in the neutral yesterday? He was taken off, of course, by a destroyer, and the only thing he said was: 'Twenty-five time I 'ave insured, but not this time... 'Ang it!"

The trawlers lunged ahead toward the forlorn neutral. Our destroyer nipped past us with that high-shouldered, terrier-like pouncing action of the newer boats, and went ahead. A tramp in ballast, her propeller half out of water, threshed along through the sallow haze.

'Lord! What a shot!' somebody said enviously. The men on the little deck looked across at the slow-moving silhouette. One of them, a cigarette behind his ear, smiled at a companion.

Then we went down--not as they go when they are pressed (the record, I believe, is 50 feet in 50 seconds from top to bottom), but genteelly, to an orchestra of appropriate sounds, roarings, and blowings, and after the orders, which come from the commander alone, utter silence and peace.

'There's the bottom. We bumped at fifty-fifty-two,' he said.

'I didn't feel it.'

'We'll try again. Watch the gauge, and you'll see it flick a little.'

The Practice Of The Art

It may have been so, but I was more interested in the faces, and above all the eyes, all down the length of her. It was to them, of course, the simplest of manoeuvres. They dropped into gear as no machine could; but the training of years and the experience of the year leaped up behind those steady eyes under the electrics in the shadow of the tall motors, between the pipes and the curved hull, or glued to their special gauges. One forgot the bodies altogether - but one will never forget the eyes or the ennobled faces. One man I remember in particular. On deck his was no more than a grave, rather striking countenance, cast in the unmistakable petty officer's mould. Below, as I saw him in profile handling a vital control, he looked like the Doge

39

of Venice, the Prior of some sternly-ruled monastic order, an old-time Pope – anything that signifies trained and stored intellectual power utterly and ascetically devoted to some vast impersonal end. And so with a much younger man, who changed into such a monk as Frank Dicksee used to draw. Only a couple of torpedo-men, not being in gear for the moment, read an illustrated paper. Their time did not come till we went up and got to business, which meant firing at our destroyer, and, I think, keeping out of the light of a friend's torpedoes.

The attack and everything connected with it is solely the commander's affair. He is the only one who gets any fun at all – since he is the eye, the brain, and the hand of the whole – this single figure at the periscope. The second in command heaves sighs, and prays that the dummy torpedo (there is less trouble about the live ones) will go off all right, or he'll be told about it. The others wait and follow the quick run of orders. It is, if not a convention, a fairly established custom that the commander shall inferentially give his world some idea of what is going on. At least, I only heard of one man who says nothing whatever, and doesn't even wriggle his shoulders when he is on the sight. The others soliloquise, etc., according to their temperament; and the periscope is as revealing as golf.

Submarines nowadays are expected to look out for themselves more than at the old practices, when the destroyers walked circumspectly. We dived and circulated under water for a while, and then rose for a sight-something like this: 'Up a little-up! Up still! Where the deuce has he got to-Ah! (Half a dozen orders as to helm and depth of descent, and a pause broken by a drumming noise somewhere above, which increases and passes away.) That's better! Up again! (This refers to the periscope.) Yes. Ah! No, we don't think! All right! Keep her down, damn it! Umm! That ought to be nineteen knots... Dirty trick!

He's changing speed. No, he isn't. He's all right. Ready forward there! (A valve sputters and drips, the torpedo-men crouch over their tubes and nod to themselves. Their faces have changed now.) He hasn't spotted us yet. We'll ju-ust-(more helm and depth orders, but specially helm) – 'Wish we were working a beam-tube. Ne'er mind! Up! (A last string of orders.) Six hundred, and he doesn't see us! Fire!'

The dummy left; the second in command cocked one ear and looked relieved. Up we rose; the wet air and spray spattered through the hatch; the destroyer swung off to retrieve the dummy.

'Careless brutes destroyers are,' said one officer. 'That fellow nearly walked over us just now. Did you notice?' The commander was playing his game out over again – stroke by stroke. 'With a beam-tube I'd ha' strafed him amidships,' he concluded.

'Why didn't you then?' I asked.

There were loads of shiny reasons, which reminded me that we were at war and cleared for action, and that the interlude had been merely play. A companion rose alongside and wanted to know whether we had seen anything of her dummy.

'No. But we heard it,' was the short answer.

I was rather annoyed, because I had seen that particular

daughter of destruction on the stocks only a short time ago, and here she was grown up and talking about her missing children!

In the harbour again, one found more submarines, all patterns and makes and sizes, with rumours of yet more and larger to follow. Naturally their men say that we are only at the beginning of the submarine. We shall have them presently for all purposes.

THE MAN AND THE WORK

Now here is a mystery of the Service.

A man gets a boat which for two years becomes his very self —

His morning hope, his evening dream,
His joy throughout the day.

With him is a second in command, an engineer, and some others. They prove each other's souls habitually every few days, by the direct test of peril, till they act, think, and endure as a unit, in and with the boat. That commander is transferred to another boat. He tries to take with him if he can, which he can't, as many of his other selves as possible. He is pitched into a new type twice the size of the old one, with three times as many gadgets, an unexplored temperament and unknown leanings. After his first trip he comes back clamouring for the

42

head of her constructor, of his own second in command, his engineer, his cox, and a few other ratings. They for their part wish him dead on the beach, because, last commission with So-and-so, nothing ever went wrong anywhere. A fortnight later you can remind the commander of what he said, and he will deny every word of it. She's not, he says, so very vile—things considered-barring her five-ton torpedo-derricks, the abominations of her wireless, and the tropical temperature of her beer-lockers. All of which signifies that the new boat has found her soul, and her commander would not change her for battle-cruisers. Therefore, that he may remember he is the Service and not a branch of it, he is after certain seasons shifted to a battle-cruiser, where he lives in a blaze of admirals and aiguillettes, responsible for vast decks and crypt-like flats, a student of extended above-water tactics, thinking in tens of thousands of yards instead of his modest but deadly three to twelve hundred.

And the man who takes his place straight-way forgets that he ever looked down on great rollers from a sixty-foot bridge under the whole breadth of heaven, but crawls and climbs and dives through conning-towers with those same waves wet in his neck, and when the cruisers pass him, tearing the deep open in half a gale, thanks God he is not as they are, and goes to bed beneath their distracted keels.

'But submarine work is cold-blooded business.'

(This was at a little session in a green-curtained 'wardroom' cum owner's cabin.)

'Then there's no truth in the yarn that you can feel when the torpedo's going to get home?' I asked.

'Not a word. You sometimes see it get home, or miss, as the case may be. Of course, it's never your fault if it misses. It's all your second-in-command.'

'That's true, too,' said the second. 'I catch it all round. That's what I am here for.'

'And what about the third man?' There was one aboard at the time.

'He generally comes from a smaller boat, to pick up real work – if he can suppress his intellect and doesn't talk 'last commission."

The third hand promptly denied the possession of any intellect, and was quite dumb about his last boat.

'And the men?'

'They train on, too. They train each other. Yes, one gets to know 'em about as well as they get to know us. Up topside, a man can take you in – take himself in - for months; for half a commission, p'rhaps. Down below he can't. It's all in cold blood--not like at the front, where they have something exciting all the time.'

'Then bumping mines isn't exciting?'

'Not one little bit. You can't bump back at 'em. Even with

a Zepp----'

'Oh, now and then,' one interrupted, and they laughed as they explained.

'Yes, that was rather funny. One of our boats came up slap underneath a low Zepp. 'Looked for the sky, you know, and couldn't see anything except this fat, shining belly almost on top of 'em. Luckily, it wasn't the Zepp's stingin' end. So our boat went to windward and kept just awash. There was a bit of a sea, and the Zepp had to work against the wind. (They don't like that.) Our boat sent a man to the gun. He was pretty well drowned, of course, but he hung on, choking and spitting, and held his breath, and got in shots where he could. This Zepp was strafing bombs about for all she was worth, and – who was it? – Macartney, I think, potting at her between dives; and naturally all hands wanted to look at the performance, so about half the North Sea flopped down below and – oh, they had a Charlie Chaplin time of it! Well, somehow, Macartney managed to rip the Zepp a bit, and she went to leeward with a list on her. We saw her a fortnight later with a patch on her port side. Oh, if Fritz only fought clean, this wouldn't be half a bad show. But Fritz can't fight clean.'

'And we can't do what he does – even if we were allowed to,' one said.

'No, we can't. 'Tisn't done. We have to fish Fritz out of the water, dry him, and give him cocktails, and send him to Donnington Hall.'

'And what does Fritz do?' I asked.

'He sputters and clicks and bows. He has all the correct

motions, you know; but, of course, when he's your prisoner you can't tell him what he really is.'

'And do you suppose Fritz understands any of it?' I went on.

'No. Or he wouldn't have lusitaniaed. This war was his first chance of making his name, and he chucked it all away for the sake of showin' off as a foul Gottstrafer.'

And they talked of that hour of the night when submarines come to the top like mermaids to get and give information; of boats whose business it is to fire as much and to splash about as aggressively as possible; and of other boats who avoid any sort of display – dumb boats watching and relieving watch, with their periscope just showing like a crocodile's eye, at the back of islands and the mouths of channels where something may some day move out in procession to its doom.

Be well assured that on our side
     Our challenged oceans fight,
Though headlong wind and heaping tide
     Make us their sport to-night.
Through force of weather, not of war,
     In jeopardy we steer.
Then, welcome Fate's discourtesy
     Whereby it shall appear
          How in all time of our distress
          As in our triumph too,
          The game is more than the player of the
               game,
          And the ship is more than the crew!

Be well assured, though wave and wind
     Have mightier blows in store,
That we who keep the watch assigned
     Must stand to it the more;
And as our streaming bows dismiss

Each billow's baulked career,
Sing, welcome Fate's discourtesy
Whereby it is made clear
How in all time of our distress
As in our triumph too,
The game is more than the player of the
game,
And the ship is more than the crew!

Be well assured, though in our power
Is nothing left to give
But time and place to meet the hour
And leave to strive to live,
Till these dissolve our Order holds,
Our Service binds us here.
Then, welcome Fate's discourtesy
Whereby it is made clear
How in all time of our distress
And our deliverance too,
The game is more than the player of the
game,
And the ship is more than the crew!

PATROLS

I

ON the edge of the North Sea sits an Admiral in charge
of a stretch of coast without lights or marks, along
which the traffic moves much as usual. In front of him there
is nothing but the east wind, the enemy, and some few our
ships. Behind him there are towns, with M.P.'s attached, who a
little while ago didn't see the reason for certain lighting orders.
When a Zeppelin or two came, they saw. Left and right of
him are enormous docks, with vast crowded sheds, miles of
stone-faced quay-edges, loaded with all manner of supplies
and crowded with mixed shipping.

In this exalted world one met Staff-Captains, Staff-
Commanders, Staff-Lieutenants, and Secretaries, with
Paymasters so senior that they almost ranked with Admirals.
There were Warrant Officers, too, who long ago gave up
splashing about decks barefoot, and now check and issue

stores to the ravenous, untruthful fleets. Said one of these, guarding a collection of desirable things, to a cross between a sick-bay attendant and a junior writer (but he was really an expert burglar), 'No! An' you can tell Mr. So-and-so, with my compliments, that the storekeeper's gone away-right away-with the key of these stores in his pocket. Understand me? In his trousers pocket.'

He snorted at my next question.

'*Do* I know any destroyer-lootenants?' said he. 'This coast's rank with 'em! Destroyer-lootenants are born stealing. It's a mercy they's too busy to practise forgery, or I'd be in gaol. Engineer-Commanders? Engineer-Lootenants? They're worse!... Look here! If my own mother was to come to me beggin' brass screws for her own coffin, I'd – I'd think twice before I'd oblige the old lady. War's war, I grant you that; but what I've got to contend with is crime.'

I referred to him a case of conscience in which every one concerned acted exactly as he should, and it nearly ended in murder. During a lengthy action, the working of a gun was hampered by some empty cartridge-cases which the lieutenant in charge made signs (no man could hear his neighbour speak just then) should be hove overboard. Upon which the gunner rushed forward and made other signs that they were 'on charge,' and must be tallied and accounted for. He, too, was trained in a strict school. Upon which the lieutenant, but that he was busy, would have slain the gunner for refusing orders in action. Afterwards he wanted him shot by court-martial. But every one was voiceless by then, and could only mouth and croak at each other, till somebody laughed, and the pedantic gunner was spared.

'Well, that's what you might fairly call a naval crux,' said my friend among the stores. 'The Lootenant was right. 'Mustn't refuse orders in action. The Gunner was right. Empty cases are on charge. No one ought to chuck 'em away that way, but... Damn it, they were all of 'em right! It ought to ha' been a marine. Then they could have killed him and preserved discipline at the same time.'

A Little Theory

The problem of this coast resolves itself into keeping touch with the enemy's movements; in preparing matters to trap and hinder him when he moves, and in so entertaining him that he shall not have time to draw clear before a blow descends on him from another quarter. There are then three lines of defence: the outer, the inner, and the home waters. The traffic and fishing are always with us.

The blackboard idea of it is always to have stronger forces more immediately available everywhere than those the enemy can send. x German submarines draw a English destroyers. Then x calls $x + y$ to deal with a, who, in turn, calls up b, a scout, and possibly a², with a fair chance that, if $x + y + z$ (a Zeppelin) carry on, they will run into $a^2 + b^2 + c$ cruisers. At this point, the equation generally stops; if it continued, it would end mathematically in the whole of the German Fleet coming out. Then another factor which we may call the Grand Fleet would come from another place. To change the comparisons: the Grand Fleet is the 'strong left' ready to give the knock-out blow on the point of the chin when the head is thrown up. The other fleets and other arrangements threaten the enemy's solar plexus and stomach. Somewhere in relation to the Grand Fleet lies the 'blockading' cordon which examines neutral traffic. It could be drawn as tight as a Turkish bowstring, but for reasons which we may arrive at after the war, it does not seem to have been so drawn up to date.

The enemy lies behind his mines, and ours, raids our coasts when he sees a chance, and kills seagoing civilians at sight or guess, with intent to terrify. Most sailor-men are mixed up with a woman or two; a fair percentage of them have seen men drown. They can realise what it is when women go down choking in horrible tangles and heavings of draperies. To say that the enemy has cut himself from the fellowship of all who use the seas is rather understating the case. As a man observed thoughtfully: 'You can't look at any water now without seeing 'Lusitania' sprawlin' all across it. And just think of those words, 'North-German Lloyd,' 'Hamburg-Amerika' and such things, in the time to come. They simply mustn't be.'

He was an elderly trawler, respectable as they make them, who, after many years of fishing, had discovered his real vocation. 'I never thought I'd like killin' men,' he reflected. 'Never seemed to be any o' my dooty. But it is – and I do!'

A great deal of the East Coast work concerns mine-fields – ours and the enemy's - both of which shift as occasion requires.

We search for and root out the enemy's mines; they do the like by us. It is a perpetual game of finding, springing, and laying traps on the least as well as the most likely runaways that ships use – such sea snaring and wiring as the world never dreamt of. We are hampered in this, because our Navy respects neutrals; and spends a great deal of its time in making their path safe for them. The enemy does not. He blows them up, because that cows and impresses them, and so adds to his prestige.

Death And The Destroyer

The easiest way of finding a mine-field is to steam into it, on the edge of night for choice, with a steep sea running, for that brings the bows down like a chopper on the detonator-horns. Some boats have enjoyed this experience and still live. There was one destroyer (and there may have been others since) who came through twenty-four hours of highly-compressed life. She had an idea that there was a mine-field somewhere about, and left her companions behind while she explored. The weather was dead calm, and she walked delicately. She saw one Scandinavian steamer blow up a couple of miles away, rescued the skipper and some hands; saw another neutral, which she could not reach till all was over, skied in another direction; and, between her life-saving efforts and her natural curiosity, got herself as thoroughly mixed up with the field as a camel among tent-ropes. A destroyer's bows are very fine, and her sides are very straight. This causes her to cleave the wave with the minimum of disturbance, and this boat had no desire to cleave anything else. None the less, from time to time, she heard a mine grate, or tinkle, or jar (I could not arrive at the precise note it strikes, but they say it is unpleasant) on her plates. Sometimes she would be free of them for a long while, and began to hope she was clear. At other times they were numerous, but when at last she seemed to have worried out of the danger zone lieutenant and sub together left the bridge for a cup of tea. ('In those days we took mines very seriously, you know.') As they were in act to drink, they heard the hateful sound again just outside the wardroom. Both put their cups down with extreme care, little fingers extended ('We felt as if they might blow up, too'), and tip-toed on deck, where they met the foc'sle also on tip-toe. They pulled themselves together, and asked severely what the foc'sle thought it was doing. 'Beg pardon, sir, but there's another of those blighters tap-tapping alongside, our end.' They all waited and listened to their common coffin being nailed by Death himself. But the things bumped away. At this point they thought it only decent to invite the rescued skipper, warm and blanketed in one of their bunks, to step up and do any further perishing in the open.

'No, thank you,' said he. 'Last time I was blown up in my bunk, too. That was all right. So I think, now, too, I stay in my bunk here. It is cold upstairs.'

Somehow or other they got out of the mess after all. 'Yes, we used to take mines awfully seriously in those days. One comfort is, Fritz'll take them seriously when he comes out.

Fritz don't like mines.'

'Who does?' I wanted to know.

'If you'd been here a little while ago, you'd seen a Commander comin' in with a big 'un slung under his counter. He brought the beastly thing in to analyse. The rest of his squadron followed at two-knot intervals, and everything in harbour that had steam up scattered.'

THE ADMIRABLE COMMANDER

Presently I had the honour to meet a Lieutenant-Commander-Admiral who had retired from the service, but, like others, had turned out again at the first flash of the guns, and now commands – he who had great ships erupting at his least signal – a squadron of trawlers for the protection of the Dogger Bank Fleet. At present prices – let alone the chance of the paying submarine – men would fish in much warmer places. His flagship was once a multi-millionaire's private yacht. In her mixture of stark, carpetless, curtainless, carbolised present, with voluptuously curved, broad-decked, easy-stairwayed past, she might be Queen Guinevere in the convent at Amesbury. And her Lieutenant-Commander, most careful to pay all due compliments to Admirals who were midshipmen when he was a Commander, leads a congregation of very hard men indeed. They do precisely what he tells them to, and with him go through strange experiences, because they love him and because his language is volcanic and wonderful – what you might call Popocatapocalyptic. I saw the Old Navy making ready to lead out the New under a grey sky and a falling glass – the wisdom and cunning of the old man backed up by the passion and power of the younger breed, and the discipline which had been his soul for half a century binding them all.

'What'll he do this time?' I asked of one who might know.

'He'll cruise between Two and Three East; but if you'll tell me what he won't do, it 'ud be more to the point! He's mine-hunting, I expect, just now.'

WASTED MATERIAL

Here is a digression suggested by the sight of a man I had known in other scenes, despatch-riding round a fleet in a petrol-launch. There are many of his type, yachtsmen of sorts accustomed to take chances, who do not hold masters' certificates and cannot be given sea-going commands. Like my friend, they do general utility work – often in their own boats. This is a waste of good material. Nobody wants amateur navigators – the traffic lanes are none too wide as it is. But these gentlemen ought to be distributed among the Trawler Fleet as strictly combatant officers. A trawler skipper may be an excellent seaman, but slow with a submarine shelling and diving, or in cutting out enemy trawlers. The young ones who can master Q.F. gun work in a very short time would--though there might be friction, a court-martial or two, and probably losses at first – pay for their keep. Even a hundred or so of amateurs, more or less controlled by their squadron commanders, would make a happy beginning, and I am sure they would all be extremely grateful.

Where the East wind is brewed fresh and
fresh every morning,
And the balmy night-breezes blow straight
from the Pole,
I heard a destroyer sing: 'What an enjoyable life
does one lead on the North Sea
Patrol!

'To blow things to bits is our business (and
Fritz's),
Which means there are mine-fields wherever
you stroll.
Unless you've particular wish to die quick,
you'll a-
void steering close to the North Sea Patrol.

We warn from disaster the mercantile
master

Who takes in high dudgeon our life-saving
rôle,
For every one's grousing at docking and
dowsing
The marks and the lights on the North
Sea Patrol.'

⁓⧓⁓

So swept but surviving, half drowned but
still driving,
I watched her head out through the swell off
the shoal,
And I heard her propellers roar: 'Write
to poor fellers
Who run such a Hell as the North Sea
Patrol!'

PATROLS

II

THE great basins were crammed with craft of kinds never known before on any Navy List. Some were as they were born, others had been converted, and a multitude have been designed for special cases. The Navy prepares against all contingencies by land, sea, and air. It was a relief to meet a batch of comprehensible destroyers and to drop again into the little mouse-trap ward-rooms, which are as large-hearted as all Our oceans. The men one used to know as destroyer-lieutenants ('born stealing') are serious Commanders and Captains today, but their sons, Lieutenants in command and Lieutenant-Commanders, do follow them. The sea in peace is a hard life; war only sketches an extra line or two round the young mouths. The routine of ships always ready for action is so part of the blood now that no one notices anything except the absence of formality and of the 'crimes' of peace. What Warrant Officers used to say at length is cut down to a grunt. What the sailor-man did not know and expected to have told him, does not exist. He has done it all too often at sea and ashore.

I watched a little party working under a leading hand at a job which, eighteen months ago, would have required a Gunner in charge. It was comic to see his orders trying to overtake the execution of them. Ratings coming aboard carried themselves with a (to me) new swing – not swank, but consciousness of adequacy. The high, dark foc'sles which, thank goodness, are only washed twice a week, received them and their bags, and they turned-to on the instant as a man picks up his life at home. Like the submarine crew, they come to be a breed apart – double-jointed, extra-toed, with brazen bowels and no sort of nerves.

It is the same in the engine-room, when the ships come in for their regular looking-over. Those who love them, which you would never guess from the language, know exactly what they need, and get it without fuss. Everything that steams has her individual peculiarity, and the great thing is, at overhaul, to keep to it and not develop a new one. If, for example, through some trick of her screws not synchronising, a destroyer always casts to port when she goes astern, do not let any zealous soul try to make her run true, or you will have to learn her helm all over again. And it is vital that you should know exactly what your ship is going to do three seconds before she does it. Similarly with men. If any one, from Lieutenant-Commander to stoker, changes his personal trick or habit – even the manner in which he clutches his chin or caresses his nose at a crisis – the matter must be carefully considered in this world where each is trustee for his neighbour's life and, vastly more important, the corporate honour.

'What are the destroyers doing just now?' I asked.

'Oh – running about – much the same as usual.'

The Navy hasn't the least objection to telling one everything that it is doing. Unfortunately, it speaks its own language, which is incomprehensible to the civilian. But you will find it all in 'The Channel Pilot' and 'The Riddle of the Sands.'

It is a foul coast, hairy with currents and rips, and mottled with shoals and rocks. Practically the same men hold on here in the same ships, with much the same crews, for months and months. A most senior officer told me that they were 'good boys' – on reflection, 'quite good boys' – but neither he nor the flags on his chart explained how they managed their lightless, unmarked navigations through black night, blinding rain, and the crazy, rebounding North Sea gales. They themselves ascribe it to Joss that they have not piled up their ships a hundred times.

'I expect it must be because we're always dodging about over the same ground. One gets to smell it. We've bumped pretty hard, of course, but we haven't expended much up to date. You never know your luck on patrol, though.'

The Nature of the Beast

Personally, though they have been true friends to me, I loathe destroyers, and all the raw, racking, ricochetting life that goes with them – the smell of the wet 'lammies' and damp wardroom cushions; the galley-chimney smoking out the bridge; the obstacle-strewn deck; and the pervading beastliness of oil, grit, and greasy iron. Even at moorings they shiver and sidle like half-backed horses. At sea they will neither rise up and fly clear like the hydroplanes, nor dive and be done with it like the submarines, but imitate the vices of both. A scientist of the lower deck describes them as: 'Half switchback, half water-chute, and Hell continuous.' Their only merit, from a landsman's point of view, is that they can crumple themselves up from stem to bridge and (I have seen it) still get home. But one does not breathe these compliments to their commanders. Other destroyers may be – they will point them out to you – poisonous bags of tricks, but their own command – never! Is she high-bowed? That is the only type which over-rides the seas instead of smothering. Is she low? Low bows glide through the water where those collier-nosed brutes smash it open. Is she mucked up with submarine-catchers? They rather improve her trim. No other ship has them. Have they been denied to her? Thank Heaven, we go to sea without a fish-curing plant on deck. Does she roll, even for her class? She is drier than Dreadnoughts. Is she permanently and infernally wet? Stiff; sir – stiff: the first requisite of a gun-platform.

'SERVICE AS REQUISITE'

Thus the Cæsars and their fortunes put out to sea with their subs and their sad-eyed engineers, and their long-suffering signalers – I do not even know the technical name of the sin which causes a man to be born a destroyer-signaller in this life – and the little yellow shells stuck all about where they can be easiest reached. The rest of their acts is written for the information of the proper authorities. It reads like a page of Todhunter. But the masters of merchant-ships could tell more of eyeless shapes, barely outlined on the foam of their own arrest, who shout orders through the thick gloom alongside. The strayed and anxious neutral knows them when their searchlights pin him across the deep, or their syrens answer the last yelp of his as steam goes out of his torpedoed boilers. They stand by to catch and soothe him in his pyjamas at the gangway, collect his scattered lifeboats, and see a warm drink into him before they turn to hunt the slayer. The drifters, punching and reeling up and down their ten-mile line of traps; the outer trawlers, drawing the very teeth of Death with water-sodden fingers, are grateful for their low, guarded signals; and when the Zeppelin's revealing star-shell cracks darkness open above him, the answering crack of the invisible destroyers' guns comforts the busy mine-layers. Big cruisers talk to them, too; and, what is more, they talk back to the cruisers. Sometimes they draw fire – pinkish spurts of light – a long way off, where Fritz is trying to coax them over a mine-field he has just laid; or they steal on Fritz in the midst of his job, and the horizon rings with barking, which the inevitable neutral who saw it all reports as 'a heavy fleet action in the North Sea.' The sea after dark can be as alive as the woods of summer nights. Everything is exactly where you don't expect it, and the shyest creatures are the farthest away from their holes. Things boom overhead like bitterns, or scutter alongside like hares, or arise dripping and hissing from below like otters. It is the destroyer's business to find out what their business may be through all the long night, and to help or hinder accordingly. Dawn sees them pitch-poling insanely between head-seas, or hanging on to bridges that sweep like scythes from one forlorn horizon to the other. A homeward-bound submarine chooses this hour to rise, very ostentatiously, and signals by hand to a lieutenant in command. (They were the same term at Dartmouth, and same first ship.)

'What's he sayin'? Secure that gun, will you? 'Can't hear oneself speak,' The gun is a bit noisy on its mountings, but that isn't the reason for the destroyer-lieutenant's short temper.

''Says he's goin' down, sir,' the signaller replies. What the submarine had spelt out, and everybody knows it, was: 'Cannot approve of this extremely frightful weather. Am going to bye-bye.'

'Well!' snaps the lieutenant to his signaller, 'what are you grinning at?' The submarine has hung on to ask if the destroyer will 'kiss her and whisper good-night.' A breaking sea smacks her tower in the middle of the insult. She closes like an oyster, but – just too late. Habet! There must be a quarter of a ton of water somewhere down below, on its way to her ticklish batteries.

'What a wag!' says the signaller, dreamily. 'Well, 'e can't say 'e didn't get 'is little kiss.'

The lieutenant in command smiles. The sea is a beast, but a just beast.

This is trivial enough, but what would you have? If Admirals will not strike the proper attitudes, nor Lieutenants emit the appropriate sentiments, one is forced back on the truth, which is that the men at the heart of the great matters in our Empire are, mostly, of an even simplicity. From the advertising point of view they are stupid, but the breed has always been stupid in this department. It may be due, as our enemies assert, to our racial snobbery, or, as others hold, to a certain God-given lack of imagination which saves us from being over-concerned at the effects of our appearances on others. Either way, it deceives the enemies' people more than any calculated lie. When you come to think of it, though the English are the worst paper-work and viva voce liars in the world, they have been rigorously trained since their early youth to live and act lies for the comfort of the society in which they move, and so for their own comfort. The result in this war is interesting.

It is no lie that at the present moment we hold all the seas in the hollow of our hands. For that reason we shuffle over them shame-faced and apologetic, making arrangements here and flagrant compromises there, in order to give substance to the lie that we have dropped fortuitously into this high seat and are looking round the world for some one to resign it to. Nor is it any lie that, had we used the Navy's bare fist instead of its gloved hand from the beginning, we could in all likelihood have shortened the war. That being so, we elected to dab and peck at and half-strangle the enemy, to let him go and choke him again. It is no lie that we continue on our inexplicable path animated, we will try to believe till other proof is given, by a cloudy idea of alleviating or mitigating something for somebody – not ourselves. [Here, of course, is where our racial snobbery comes in, which makes the German gibber. I cannot understand why he has not accused us to our Allies of having secret commercial understandings with him.] For that reason, we shall finish the German eagle as the merciful lady killed the chicken. It took her the whole afternoon, and then, you will remember, the carcase had to be thrown away.

Meantime, there is a large and unlovely water, inhabited by plain men in severe boats, who endure cold, exposure, wet, and monotony almost as heavy as their responsibilities. Charge them with heroism – but that needs heroism, indeed! Accuse them of patriotism, they become ribald. Examine into the records of the miraculous work they have done and are doing. They will assist you, but with perfect sincerity they will make as light of the valour and fore-thought shown as of the ends they have gained for mankind. The Service takes all work for granted. It knew long ago that certain things would have to be done, and it did its best to be ready for them. When it disappeared over the sky-line for manoeuvres it was practicing – always practising; trying its men and stuff and throwing out what could not take the strain. That is why, when war came, only a few names had to be changed, and those chiefly for the sake of the body, not of the spirit. And the Seniors who hold the key to our plans and know what will be done if things happen, and what lines wear thin in the many chains, they are of one fibre and speech with the Juniors and the lower deck and all the rest who come out of the undemonstrative households ashore. 'Here is the situation as it exists now,' say the Seniors. 'This is what we do to meet it. Look and count and measure and judge for yourself, and then you will know.'

It is a safe offer. The civilian only sees that the sea is a vast place, divided between wisdom and chance. He only knows that the uttermost oceans have been swept clear, and the trade-routes purged, one by one, even as our armies were being convoyed along them; that there was no island nor key left unsearched on any waters that might hide an enemy's craft between the Arctic Circle and the Horn. He only knows that less than a day's run to the eastward of where he stands, the enemy's fleets have been held for a year and four months, in order that civilisation may go about its business on all our waters.

TALES OF 'THE TRADE'

1916

'THE TRADE'

They bear, in place of classic names,
    Letters and numbers on their skin.
They play their grisly blindfold games
    In little boxes made of tin.
Sometimes they stalk the Zeppelin,
    Sometimes they learn where mines are laid
Or where the Baltic ice is thin.
    That is the custom of 'The Trade.'

Few prize-courts sit upon their claims.
    They seldom tow their targets in.
They follow certain secret aims
    Down under, far from strife or din.
When they are ready to begin
    No flag is flown, no fuss is made

More than the shearing of a pin.
   That is the custom of 'The Trade.'
The Scout's quadruple funnel flames
   A mark from Sweden to the Swin,
The Cruiser's thundrous screw proclaims
   Her comings out and goings in:
   But only whiffs of paraffin
Or creamy rings that fizz and fade
   Show where the one-eyed Death has been.
That is the custom of 'The Trade.'

Their feats, their fortunes and their fames
   Are hidden from their nearest kin;
No eager public backs or blames,
   No journal prints the yarns they spin
   (The Censor would not let it in!)
When they return from run or raid.
   Unheard they work, unseen they win.
That is the custom of 'The Trade.'

SOME WORK IN THE BALTIC

I

NO one knows how the title of 'The Trade' came to be applied to the Submarine Service. Some say that the cruisers invented it because they pretend that submarine officers look like unwashed chauffeurs. Others think it sprang forth by itself, which means that it was coined by the Lower Deck, where they always have the proper names for things. Whatever the truth, the Submarine Service is now 'the trade'; and if you ask them why, they will answer: 'What else could you call it? The Trade's 'the trade,' of course.'

It is a close corporation; yet it recruits its men and officers from every class that uses the sea and engines, as well as from many classes that never expected to deal with either. It takes them; they disappear for a while and return changed to their very souls, for the Trade lives in a world without precedents, of which no generation has had any previous experience – a world still being made and enlarged daily. It creates and settles its own problems as it goes along, and if it cannot help itself no one else can. So the Trade lives in the dark and thinks out inconceivable and impossible things which it afterwards puts into practice.

It keeps books, too, as honest traders should. They are almost as bald as ledgers, and are written up, hour by hour, on a little sliding table that pulls out from beneath the commander's bunk. In due time they go to my Lords of the Admiralty, who presently circulate a few carefully watered extracts for the confidential information of the junior officers of the Trade, that these may see what things are done and how. The juniors read but laugh. They have heard the stories, with all the flaming detail and much of the language, either from a chief actor while they perched deferentially on the edge of a mess-room fender, or from his subordinate, in which case they were not so deferential, or from some returned member of the crew present on the occasion, who, between half-shut teeth at the wheel, jerks out what really happened. There is very little going on in the Trade that the Trade does not know within a reasonable time. But the outside world must wait until my Lords of the Admiralty release the records. Some of them have been released now.

SUBMARINE AND ICE-BREAKER

Let us take, almost at random, an episode in the life of H.M. Submarine E9. It is true that she was commanded by Commander Max Horton, but the utter impersonality of the

73

tale makes it as though the boat herself spoke. (Also, never having met or seen any of the gentlemen concerned in the matter, the writer can be impersonal too.) Some time ago, E9 was in the Baltic, in the deeps of winter, where she used to be taken to her hunting grounds by an ice-breaker. Obviously a submarine cannot use her sensitive nose to smash heavy ice with, so the broad-beamed pushing chaperone comes along to see her clear of the thick harbour and shore ice. In the open sea apparently she is left to her own devices. In company of the ice-breaker, then, E9 'proceeded' (neither in the Senior nor the Junior Service does any one officially 'go' anywhere) to a 'certain position.'

Here – it is not stated in the book, but the Trade knows every aching, single detail of what is left out – she spent a certain time in testing arrangements and apparatus, which may or may not work properly when immersed in a mixture of block-ice and dirty ice-cream in a temperature well towards zero. This is a pleasant job, made the more delightful by the knowledge that if you slip off the superstructure the deadly Baltic chill will stop your heart long before even your heavy clothes can drown you. Hence (and this is not in the book either) the remark of the highly trained sailor-man in these latitudes who, on being told by his superior officer in the execution of his duty to go to Hell, did insubordinately and enviously reply: 'D'you think I'd be here if I could?' Whereby he caused the entire personnel, beginning with the Commander, to say 'Amen,' or words to that effect. E9 evidently made things work.

Next day she reports: 'As circumstances were favourable

decided to attempt to bag a destroyer.' Her 'certain position' must have been near a well-used destroyer-run, for shortly afterwards she sees three of them, but too far off to attack, and later, as the light is failing, a fourth destroyer towards which she manoeuvres. 'Depth-keeping,' she notes, 'very difficult owing to heavy swell.' An observation balloon on a gusty day is almost as stable as a submarine 'pumping' in a heavy swell, and since the Baltic is shallow, the submarine runs the chance of being let down with a whack on the bottom. None the less, E9 works her way to within 600 yards of the quarry; fires and waits just long enough to be sure that her torpedo is running straight, and that the destroyer is holding her course. Then she 'dips to avoid detection.' The rest is deadly simple: 'At the correct moment after firing, 45 to 50 seconds, heard the unmistakable noise of torpedo detonating.' Four minutes later she rose and 'found destroyer had disappeared.' Then, for reasons probably connected with other destroyers, who, too, may have heard that unmistakable sound, she goes to bed below in the chill dark till it is time to turn homewards. When she rose she met storm from the north and logged it accordingly. 'Spray froze as it struck, and bridge became a mass of ice. Experienced considerable difficulty in keeping the conning-tower hatch free from ice. Found it necessary to keep a man continuously employed on this work. Bridge screen immovable, ice six inches thick on it. Telegraphs frozen.' In this state she forges ahead till midnight, and any one who pleases can imagine the thoughts of the continuous employee scraping and hammering round the hatch, as well as the delight of his friends below when the ice-slush spattered down the conning-tower. At last she considered it 'advisable to free the boat of ice, so went below.'

'As Requisite'

In the Senior Service the two words 'as requisite' cover everything that need not be talked about. E9 next day 'proceeded as requisite' through a series of snowstorms and recurring deposits of ice on the bridge till she got in touch with her friend the ice-breaker; and in her company ploughed and rooted her way back to the work we know. There is nothing to show that it was a near thing for E9, but somehow one has the idea that the ice-breaker did not arrive any too soon for E9's comfort and progress. (But what happens in the Baltic when the ice-breaker does not arrive?)

That was in winter. In summer quite the other way, E9 had to go to bed by day very often under the long-lasting northern light when the Baltic is as smooth as a carpet, and one cannot get within a mile and a half of anything with eyes in its head without being put down. There was one time when E9, evidently on information received, took up 'a certain position' and reported the sea 'glassy.' She had to suffer in silence, while three heavily laden German ships went by; for an attack would have given away her position. Her reward came next day, when she sighted (the words run like Marryat's) 'enemy squadron coming up fast from eastward, proceeding inshore of us.' They were two heavy battleships with an escort of destroyers, and

E9 turned to attack. She does not say how she crept up in that smooth sea within a quarter of a mile of the leading ship, 'a three-funnel ship, of either the Deutschland or Braunschweig class,' but she managed it, and fired both bow torpedoes at her.

'No. 1 torpedo was seen and heard to strike her just before foremost funnel: smoke and débris appeared to go as high as masthead.' That much E9 saw before one of the guardian destroyers ran at her. 'So,' says she, 'observing her I took my periscope off the battleship.' This was excusable, as the destroyer was coming up with intent to kill and E9 had to flood her tanks and get down quickly. Even so, the destroyer only just missed her, and she struck bottom in 43 feet. 'But,' says E9, who, if she could not see, kept her ears open, 'at the correct interval (the 45 or 50 seconds mentioned in the previous case) the second torpedo was heard to explode, though not actually seen.' E9 came up twenty minutes later to make sure. The destroyer was waiting for her a couple of hundred yards away, and again E9 dipped for the life, but 'just had time to see one large vessel approximately four or five miles away.'

Putting courage aside, think for a moment of the mere drill of it all – that last dive for that attack on the chosen battleship; the eye at the periscope watching 'No. 1 torpedo' get home; the rush of the vengeful destroyer; the instant orders for flooding everything; the swift descent which had to be arranged for with full knowledge of the shallow sea-floors waiting below, and a guess at the course that might be taken by the seeking bows above, for assuming a destroyer to draw 10 feet and a submarine on the bottom to stand 25 feet to the top of her conning-tower, there is not much clearance in 43 feet salt water, specially if the boat jumps when she touches bottom. And through all these and half a hundred other simultaneous considerations, imagine the trained minds below, counting, as only torpedo-men can count, the run of the merciless seconds that should tell when that second shot arrived. Then 'at the correct interval' as laid down in the table of distances, the boom and the jar of No. 2 torpedo, the relief, the exhaled breath and untightened lips; the impatient waiting for a second peep, and when that had been taken and the eye at the periscope had reported one little nigger-boy in place of two on the waters, perhaps cigarettes, &c., while the destroyer sickled about at a venture overhead.

Certainly they give men rewards for doing such things, but what reward can there be in any gift of Kings or peoples to match the enduring satisfaction of having done them, not alone, but with and through and by trusty and proven companions?

Defeated By Darkness

E1, also a Baltic boat, her Commander F.N. Laurence, had her experiences too. She went out one summer day and late – too late – in the evening sighted three transports. The first she hit. While she was arranging for the second, the third inconsiderately tried to ram her before her sights were on. So it was necessary to go down at once and waste whole minutes of the precious scanting light. When she rose, the stricken ship was sinking and shortly afterwards blew up. The other two were patrolling near by. It would have been a fair chance in daylight, but the darkness defeated her and she had to give up the attack.

It was E1 who during thick weather came across a squadron of battle-cruisers and got in on a flanking ship – probably the Moltke. The destroyers were very much on the alert, and she had to dive at once to avoid one who only missed her by a few feet. Then the fog shut down and stopped further developments. Thus do time and chance come to every man.

The Trade has many stories, too, of watching patrols when a boat must see chance after chance go by under her nose and write – merely write – what she has seen. Naturally they do not appear in any accessible records. Nor, which is a pity, do the authorities release the records of glorious failures, when everything goes wrong; when torpedoes break surface and squatter like ducks; or arrive full square with a clang and burst of white water and – fail to explode; when the devil is in charge of all the motors, and clutches develop play that would scare a shore-going mechanic bald; when batteries begin to give off death instead of power, and atop of all, ice or wreckage of the strewn seas racks and wrenches the hull till the whole leaking bag of tricks limps home on six missing cylinders and one ditto propeller, *plus* the indomitable will of the red-eyed husky scarecrows in charge.

There might be worse things in this world for decent people to read than such records.

BUSINESS IN THE SEA
OF MARMARA

II

THIS war is like an iceberg. We, the public, only see an eighth of it above water. The rest is out of sight and, as with the berg, one guesses its extent by great blocks that break off and shoot up to the surface from some underlying out-running spur a quarter of a mile away. So with this war sudden tales come to light which reveal unsuspected activities in unexpected quarters. One takes it for granted such things are always going on somewhere, but the actual emergence of the record is always astonishing.

Once upon a time, there were certain E type boats who worked the Sea of Marmara with thoroughness and humanity; for the two, in English hands, are compatible. The road to their hunting-grounds was strewn with peril, the waters they inhabited full of eyes that gave them no rest, and what they lost or expended in wear and tear of the chase could not be made good till they had run the gauntlet to their base again. The full tale of their improvisations and 'makee-does' will probably never come to light, though fragments can be picked up at intervals in the proper places as the men concerned come and go. The Admiralty gives only the bones, but those are not so dry, of the boat's official story.

When E14, Commander E. Courtney-Boyle, went to her work in the Sea of Marmara, she, like her sister, 'proceeded' on her gas-engine up the Dardanelles; and a gas-engine by night between steep cliffs has been described by the Lower-deck as a 'full brass band in a railway cutting.' So a fort picked her up with a searchlight and missed her with artillery. She dived under the minefield that guarded the Straits, and when she rose at dawn in the narrowest part of the channel, which is about one mile and a half across, all the forts fired at her. The water, too, was thick with steamboat patrols, out of which E14 selected a Turkish gunboat and gave her a torpedo. She had just time to see the great column of water shoot as high as the gunboat's mast when she had to dip again as 'the men in a small steamboat were leaning over trying to catch hold of the top of my periscope.'

'SIX HOURS OF BLIND DEATH'

This sentence, which might have come out of a French exercise book, is all Lieutenant-Commander Courtney-Boyle sees fit to tell, and that officer will never understand why one taxpayer at least demands his arrest after the war till he shall have given the full tale. Did he sight the shadowy underline

81

of the small steamboat green through the deadlights? Or did she suddenly swim into his vision from behind, and obscure, without warning, his periscope with a single brown clutching hand? Was she alone, or one of a mob of splashing, shouting small craft? He may well have been too busy to note, for there were patrols all around him, a minefield of curious design and undefined area somewhere in front, and steam trawlers vigorously sweeping for him astern and ahead. And when E14 had burrowed and bumped and scraped through six hours of blind death, she found the Sea of Marmara crawling with craft, and was kept down almost continuously and grew hot and stuffy in consequence. Nor could she charge her batteries in peace, so at the end of another hectic, hunted day of starting them up and breaking off and diving – which is bad for the temper – she decided to quit those infested waters near the coast and charge up somewhere off the traffic routes.

This accomplished, after a long, hot run, which did the motors no good, she went back to her beat, where she picked up three destroyers convoying a couple of troopships. But it was a glassy calm and the destroyers 'came for me.' She got off a long-range torpedo at one transport, and ducked before she could judge results. She apologises for this on the grounds that one of her periscopes had been damaged – not, as one would expect, by the gentleman leaning out of the little steamboat, but by some casual shot – calibre not specified – the day before. 'And so,' says E14, 'I could not risk my remaining one being bent.' However, she heard a thud, and the depth-gauges – those great clock-hands on the white-faced circles – 'flicked,' which is another sign of dreadful certainty down under. When she rose again she saw a destroyer convoying one burning transport to the nearest beach.

That afternoon she met a sister-boat (now gone to Valhalla), who told her that she was almost out of torpedoes, and they arranged a rendezvous for next day, but 'before we could communicate we had to dive, and I did not see her again.' There must be many such meetings in the Trade, under all skies – boat rising beside boat at the point agreed upon for interchange of news and materials; the talk shouted aloud with the speakers' eyes always on the horizon and all hands standing by to dive, even in the middle of a sentence.

Annoying Patrol Ships

E14 kept to her job, on the edge of the procession of traffic. Patrol vessels annoyed her to such an extent that 'as I had not seen any transports lately I decided to sink a patrol-ship as they were always firing on me.' So she torpedoed a thing that looked like a mine-layer, and must have been something of that kidney, for it sank in less than a minute. A tramp-steamer lumbering across the dead flat sea was thoughtfully headed back to Constantinople by firing rifles ahead of her. 'Under fire the whole day,' E14 observes philosophically. The nature of her work made this inevitable. She was all among the patrols, which kept her down a good deal and made her draw on her batteries, and when she rose to charge, watchers ashore burned oil-flares on the beach or made smokes among the hills according to the light. In either case there would be a general rush of patrolling craft of all kinds, from steam launches to gunboats. Nobody loves the Trade, though E14 did several things which made her popular. She let off a string of very surprised dhows (they were empty) in charge of a tug which promptly fled back to Constantinople; stopped a couple of steamers full of refugees, also bound for Constantinople, who were 'very pleased at being allowed to proceed' instead of being lusitaniaed as they had expected. Another refugee-boat, fleeing from goodness knows what horror, she chased into Rodosto Harbour, where, though she could not see any troops, 'they opened a heavy rifle fire on us, hitting the boat several times. So I went away and chased two more small tramps who returned towards Constantinople.'

Transports, of course, were fair game, and in spite of the necessity she was under of not risking her remaining eye, E14 got a big one in a night of wind and made another hurriedly beach itself, which then opened fire on her, assisted by the local population. 'Returned fire and proceeded,' says E14. The diversion of returning fire is one much appreciated by the lower-deck as furnishing a pleasant break in what otherwise might be a monotonous and odoriferous task. There is no drill laid down for this evolution, but etiquette and custom prescribe that on going up the hatch you shall not too energetically prod the next man ahead with the muzzle of your rifle. Likewise, when descending in quick time before the hatch closes, you are requested not to jump directly on the head of the next below.

Otherwise you act 'as requisite' on your own initiative.

When she had used up all her torpedoes E14 prepared to go home by the way she had come – there was no other – and was chased towards Gallipoli by a mixed pack composed of a gunboat, a torpedo-boat, and a tug. 'They shepherded me to Gallipoli, one each side of me and one astern, evidently expecting me to be caught by the nets there.' She walked very delicately for the next eight hours or so, all down the Straits, underrunning the strong tides, ducking down when the fire from the forts got too hot, verifying her position and the position of the minefield, but always taking notes of every ship in sight, till towards teatime she saw our Navy off the entrance and 'rose to the surface abeam of a French battleship who gave us a rousing cheer.' She had been away, as nearly as possible, three weeks, and a kind destroyer escorted her to the base, where we will leave her for the moment while we consider the performance of E11 (Lieutenant-Commander M.E. Nasmith) in the same waters at about the same season.

E11 'proceeded' in the usual way, to the usual accompaniments of hostile destroyers, up the Straits, and meets the usual difficulties about charging-up when she gets through. Her wireless naturally takes this opportunity to give trouble, and E11 is left, deaf and dumb, somewhere in the middle of the Sea of Marmara, diving to avoid hostile destroyers in the intervals of trying to come at the fault in her aerial. (Yet it is noteworthy that the language of the Trade, though technical, is no more emphatic or incandescent than that of top-side ships.)

Then she goes towards Constantinople, finds a Turkish

torpedo-gunboat off the port, sinks her, has her periscope smashed by a six-pounder, retires, fits a new top on the periscope, and at 10.30 A.M. – they must have needed it – pipes 'All hands to bathe.' Much refreshed, she gets her wireless linked up at last, and is able to tell the authorities where she is and what she is after.

Mr. Silas Q. Swing

At this point – it was off Rodosto – enter a small steamer which does not halt when requested, and so is fired at with 'several rounds' from a rifle. The crew, on being told to abandon her, tumble into their boats with such haste that they capsize two out of three. 'Fortunately,' says E11, 'they are able to pick up everybody.' You can imagine to yourself the confusion alongside, the raffle of odds and ends floating out of the boats, and the general parti-coloured hurrah's-nest all over the bright broken water. What you cannot imagine is this: 'An American gentleman then appeared on the upper deck who informed us that his name was Silas Q. Swing, of the *Chicago Sun*, and that he was pleased to make our acquaintance. He then informed us that the steamer was proceeding to Chanak and he wasn't sure if there were any stores aboard.' If anything could astonish the Trade at this late date, one would almost fancy that the apparition of Silas Q. Swing ('very happy to meet you, gentlemen') might have started a rivet or two on E11's placid skin. But she never even quivered. She kept a lieutenant of the name of D'Oyley Hughes, an expert in demolition parties;

and he went aboard the tramp and reported any quantity of stores – a six-inch gun, for instance, lashed across the top of the forehatch (Silas Q. Swing must have been an unobservant journalist), a six-inch gun-mounting in the forehold, pedestals for twelve-pounders thrown in as dunnage, the afterhold full of six-inch projectiles, and a scattering of other commodities. They put the demolition charge well in among the six-inch stuff, and she took it all to the bottom in a few minutes, after being touched off.

'Simultaneously with the sinking of the vessel,' the E11 goes on, 'smoke was observed to the eastward.' It was a steamer who had seen the explosion and was running for Rodosto. E11 chased her till she tied up to Rodosto pier, and then torpedoed her where she lay – a heavily laden store-ship piled high with packing-cases. The water was shallow here, and though E11 bumped along the bottom, which does not make for steadiness of aim, she was forced to show a good deal of her only periscope, and had it dented, but not damaged by rifle-fire from the beach. As she moved out of Rodosto Bay she saw a paddle-boat loaded with barbed wire, which stopped on the hail, but 'as we ranged alongside her, attempted to ram us, but failed owing to our superior speed.' Then she ran for the beach 'very skilfully,' keeping her stern to E11 till she drove ashore beneath some cliffs. The demolition-squad were just getting to work when 'a party of horsemen appeared on the cliffs above and opened a hot fire on the conning tower.' E11 got out, but owing to the shoal water it was some time before she could get under enough to fire a torpedo. The stern of a stranded paddle-boat is no great target and the thing exploded on the beach. Then she 'recharged batteries and proceeded slowly on the surface towards Constantinople.' All this between the ordinary office hours of 10 A.M. and 4 P.M.

Her next day's work opens, as no pallid writer of fiction dare begin, thus: 'Having dived unobserved into Constantinople, observed, etc.' Her observations were rather hampered by cross-tides, mud, and currents, as well as the vagaries of one of her own torpedoes which turned upside down and ran about promiscuously. It hit something at last, and so did another shot that she fired, but the waters by Constantinople Arsenal are not healthy to linger in after one has scared up the whole sea-front, so 'turned to go out.' Matters were a little better below, and E11 in her perilous passage might have been a lady of the harem tied up in a sack and thrown into the Bosporus. She grounded heavily; she bounced up 30 feet, was headed down again by a manoeuvre easier to shudder over than to describe, and when she came to rest on the bottom found herself being swivelled right round the compass. They watched the compass with much interest. 'It was concluded, therefore, that the vessel (E11 is one of the few who speaks of herself as a 'vessel' as well as a 'boat') was resting on the shoal under the Leander Tower, and was being turned round by the current.' So they corrected her, started the motors, and 'bumped gently down into 85 feet of water' with no more knowledge than the lady in the sack where the next bump would land them.

And the following day was spent 'resting in the centre of the Sea of Marmara.' That was their favourite preening perch between operations, because it gave them a chance to tidy the boat and bathe, and they were a cleanly people both in their methods and their persons. When they boarded a craft and found nothing of consequence they 'parted with many expressions of good will,' and E11 'had a good wash. She gives her reasons at length; for going in and out of Constantinople and the Straits is all in the day's work, but going dirty, you understand, is serious. She had 'of late noticed the atmosphere in the boat becoming very oppressive, the reason doubtless being that there was a quantity of dirty linen aboard, and also the scarcity of fresh water necessitated a limit being placed on the frequency of personal washing.' Hence the centre of the Sea of Marmara; all hands playing overside and as much laundry work as time and the Service allowed. One of the reasons, by the way, why we shall be good friends with the Turk again is that he has many of our ideas about decency.

In due time E11 went back to her base. She had discovered a way of using unspent torpedoes twice over, which surprised the enemy, and she had as nearly as possible been cut down by a ship which she thought was running away from her. Instead of which (she made the discovery at three thousand yards, both craft all out) the stranger steamed straight at her. 'The enemy then witnessed a somewhat spectacular dive at full speed from the surface to 20 feet in as many seconds. He then really did turn tail and was seen no more.' Going through the Straits she observed an empty troopship at anchor, but reserved her torpedoes in the hope of picking up some battleships lower down. Not finding these in the Narrows, she nosed her way back and sank the trooper, 'afterwards continuing journey down the Straits.' Off Kilid Bahr something happened; she got out of trim and had to be fully flooded before she could be brought to her required depth. It might have been whirlpools under water, or – other things. (They tell a story of a boat which once went mad in these very waters, and for no reason ascertainable from within plunged to depths that contractors do not allow for; rocketed up again like a swordfish, and would doubtless have so continued till she died, had not something she had fouled dropped off and let her recover her composure.)

An hour later: 'Heard a noise similar to grounding. Knowing this to be impossible in the water in which the boat then was, I came up to 20 feet to investigate, and observed a large mine preceding the periscope at a distance of about 20 feet, which was apparently hung up by its moorings to the port hydroplane.' Hydroplanes are the fins at bow and stern which regulate a submarine's diving. A mine weighs anything from hundredweights to half-tons. Sometimes it explodes if you merely think about it; at others you can batter it like an empty sardine-tin and it submits meekly; but at no time is it meant to wear on a hydroplane. They dared not come up to unhitch it, 'owing to the batteries ashore,' so they pushed the dim shape ahead of them till they got outside Kum Kale. They then went full astern, and emptied the after-tanks, which brought the bows down, and in this posture rose to the surface, when 'the rush of water from the screws together with the sternway gathered allowed the mine to fall clear of the vessel.'

Now a fool, said Dr. Johnson, would have tried to describe that.

Ravages And Repairs

III

BEFORE we pick up the further adventures of H.M. Submarine E14 and her partner E11, here is what you might call a cutting-out affair in the Sea of Marmara which E12 (Lieutenant-Commander K.M. Bruce) put through quite on the old lines.

E12's main motors gave trouble from the first, and she seems to have been a cripple for most of that trip. She sighted two small steamers, one towing two, and the other three, sailing vessels; making seven keels in all. She stopped the first steamer, noticed she carried a lot of stores, and, moreover, that her crew – she had no boats – were all on deck in life-belts. Not seeing any gun, E12 ran up alongside and told the first lieutenant to board. The steamer then threw a bomb at E12, which struck, but luckily did not explode, and opened fire on the boarding-party with rifles and a concealed 1-in. gun. E12 answered with her six-pounder, and also with rifles. The two sailing ships in tow, very properly, tried to foul E12's propellers and 'also opened fire with rifles.'

It was as Orientally mixed a fight as a man could wish: The first lieutenant and the boarding-party engaged on the steamer, E12 foul of the steamer, and being fouled by the sailing ships; the six-pounder methodically perforating the steamer from bow to stern; the steamer's 1-in. gun and the rifles from the sailing ships raking everything and everybody else; E12's coxswain on the conning-tower passing up ammunition; and E12's one workable motor developing 'slight defects' at, of course, the moment when power to manoeuvre was vital.

The account is almost as difficult to disentangle as the actual mess must have been. At any rate, the six-pounder caused an explosion in the steamer's ammunition, whereby the steamer sank in a quarter of an hour, giving time – and a hot time it must have been – for E12 to get clear of her and to sink the two sailing ships. She then chased the second steamer, who slipped her three tows and ran for the shore. E12 knocked her about a good deal with gun-fire as she fled, saw her drive on the beach well alight, and then, since the beach opened fire with a gun at 1500 yards, went away to retinker her motors and write up her log. She approved of her first lieutenant's behaviour 'under very trying circumstances' (this probably refers to the explosion of the ammunition by the six-pounder which, doubtless, jarred the boarding-party) and of the cox who acted as ammunition-hoist; and of the gun's crew, who 'all did very well' under rifle and small-gun fire 'at a range of about ten yards.' But she never says what she really said about her motors.

A Brawl At A Pier

Now we will take E14 on various work, either alone
or as flagship of a squadron composed of herself and
Lieutenant-Commander Nasmith's boat, E11. Hers was a busy
midsummer, and she came to be intimate with all sort of craft
– such as the two-funnelled gunboat off Sar Kioi, who 'fired
at us, and missed as usual'; hospital ships going back and forth
unmolested to Constantinople; 'the gunboat which fired at me
on Sunday,' and other old friends, afloat and ashore.

When the crew of the Turkish brigantine full of stores got
into their boats by request, and then 'all stood up and cursed
us,' E14 did not lose her temper, even though it was too rough
to lie alongside the abandoned ship. She told Acting Lieutenant
R.W. Lawrence, of the Royal Naval Reserve, to swim off to
her, which he did, and after a 'cursory search' – Who can be
expected to Sherlock Holmes for hours with nothing on? – set
fire to her 'with the aid of her own matches and paraffin oil.'

Then E14 had a brawl with a steamer with a yellow funnel,
blue top and black band, lying at a pier among dhows. The
shore took a hand in the game with small guns and rifles, and,
as E14 manoeuvred about the roadstead 'as requisite' there
was a sudden unaccountable explosion which strained her very
badly. 'I think,' she muses, 'I must have caught the moorings
of a mine with my tail as I was turning, and exploded it. It is
possible that it might have been a big shell bursting over us,
but I think this unlikely, as we were 30 feet at the time.' She
is always a philosophical boat, anxious to arrive at the reason

of facts, and when the game is against her she admits it freely.

There was nondescript craft of a few hundred tons, who 'at a distance did not look very warlike,' but when chased suddenly played a couple of six-pounders and 'got off two dozen rounds at us before we were under. Some of them were only about 20 yards off.' And when a wily steamer, after sidling along the shore, lay up in front of a town she became 'indistinguishable from the houses,' and so was safe because we do not löwestrafe open towns.

Sailing dhows full of grain had to be destroyed. At one rendezvous, while waiting for E11, E14 dealt with three such cases and then 'towed the crews inshore and gave them biscuits, beef, and rum and water, as they were rather wet.' Passenger steamers were allowed to proceed, because they were 'full of people of both sexes,' which is an unkultured way of doing business.

Here is another instance of our insular type of mind. An empty dhow is passed which E14 was going to leave alone, but it occurs to her that the boat looks 'rather deserted,' and she fancies she sees two heads in the water. So she goes back half a mile, picks up a couple of badly exhausted men, frightened out of their wits, gives them food and drink, and puts them aboard their property. Crews that jump overboard have to be picked up, even if, as happened in one case, there are twenty of them and one of them is a German bank manager taking a quantity of money to the Chanak Bank. Hospital ships are carefully looked over as they come and go, and are left to their own devices; but they are rather a nuisance because they force

E14 and others to dive for them when engaged in stalking warrantable game. There were a good many hospital ships, and as far as we can make out they all played fair. E11 boarded one and 'reported everything satisfactory.'

STRANGE MESSMATES

A layman cannot tell from the reports which of the duties demanded the most work – whether the continuous clearing out of transports, dhows, and sailing ships, generally found close to the well-gunned and attentive beach, or the equally continuous attacks on armed vessels of every kind. Whatever else might be going on, there was always the problem how to arrange for the crews of sunk ships. If a dhow has no small boats, and you cannot find one handy, you have to take the crew aboard, where they are horribly in the way, and add to the oppressiveness of the atmosphere – like 'the nine people, including two very old men,' whom E14 made honorary members of her mess for several hours till she could put them ashore after dark. Oddly enough she 'could not get anything out of them.' Imagine nine bewildered Moslems suddenly decanted into the reeking clamorous bowels of a fabric obviously built by Shaitan himself, and surrounded by – but our people are people of the Book and not dog-eating Kaffirs, and I will wager a great deal that that little company went ashore in better heart and stomach than when they were passed down the conning-tower hatch.

Then there were queer amphibious battles with troops who had to be shelled as they marched towards Gallipoli along the coast roads. E14 went out with E11 on this job, early one morning, each boat taking her chosen section of landscape. Thrice E14 rose to fire, thinking she saw the dust of feet, but 'each time it turned out to be bullocks.' When the shelling was ended 'I think the troops marching along that road must have been delayed and a good many killed.' The Turks got up a field-gun in the course of the afternoon – your true believer never hurries – which out-ranged both boats, and they left accordingly.

The next day she changed billets with E11, who had the luck to pick up and put down a battleship close to Gallipoli. It turned out to be the *Barbarossa*. Meantime E14 got a 5000-ton supply ship, and later had to burn a sailing ship loaded with 200 bales of leaf and cut tobacco – Turkish tobacco! Small wonder that E11 'came alongside that afternoon and remained for an hour' – probably making cigarettes.

Refitting Under Difficulties

Then E14 went back to her base. She had a hellish time among the Dardanelles nets; was, of course, fired at by the forts, just missed a torpedo from the beach, scraped a mine, and when she had time to take stock found electric mine-wires twisted round her propellers and all her hull scraped and scored with wire marks. But that, again, was only in the day's work. The point she insisted upon was that she had been for seventy days in the Sea of Marmara with no securer base for refit than the centre of the same, and during all that while she had not had 'any engine-room defect which has not been put right by the engine-room staff of the boat.' The commander and the third officer went sick for a while; the first lieutenant got gastro-enteritis and was in bed (if you could see that bed!) 'for the remainder of our stay in the Sea of Marmara,' but 'this boat has never been out of running order.' The credit is ascribed to 'the excellence of my chief engine-room artificer, James Hollier Hague, O.N. 227715,' whose name is duly submitted to the authorities 'for your consideration for advancement to the rank of warrant officer.'

Seventy days of every conceivable sort of risk, within and without, in a boat which is all engine-room, except where she is sick-bay; twelve thousand miles covered since last overhaul and 'never out of running order'– thanks to Mr. Hague. Such artists as he are the kind of engine-room artificers that commanders intrigue to get hold of – each for his own boat – and when the tales are told in the Trade, their names, like Abou Ben Adhem's, lead all the rest.

I do not know the exact line of demarcation between engine-room and gunnery repairs, but I imagine it is faint and fluid. E11, for example, while she was helping E14 to shell a beached steamer, smashed half her gun-mounting, 'the gun-layer being thrown overboard, and the gun nearly following him.' However, the mischief was repaired in the next twenty-four hours, which, considering the very limited deck space of a submarine, means that all hands must have been moderately busy. One hopes that they had not to dive often during the job.

But worse is to come. E2 (Commander D. Stocks) carried an externally mounted gun which, while she was diving up the Dardanelles on business, got hung up in the wires and stays of a net. She saw them through the conning-tower scuttles at a depth of 80 ft – one wire hawser round the gun, another round the conning-tower, and so on. There was a continuous crackling of small explosions overhead which she thought were charges aimed at her by the guard-boats who watch the nets. She considered her position for a while, backed, got up steam, barged ahead, and shore through the whole affair in one wild surge. Imagine the roof of a navigable cottage after it has snapped telegraph lines with its chimney, and you will get a small idea of what happens to the hull of a submarine when she uses her gun to break wire hawsers with.

Trouble With A Gun

E2 was a wet, strained, and uncomfortable boat for the rest of her cruise. She sank steamers, burned dhows; was worried by torpedo-boats and hunted by Hun planes; hit bottom freely and frequently; silenced forts that fired at her from lonely beaches; warned villages who might have joined in the game that they had better keep to farming; shelled railway lines and stations; would have shelled a pier, but found there was a hospital built at one end of it, 'so could not bombard';

came upon dhows crowded with 'female refugees' which she 'allowed to proceed,' and was presented with fowls in return; but through it all her chief preoccupation was that racked and strained gun and mounting. When there was nothing else doing she reports sourly that she 'worked on gun.' As a philosopher of the lower deck put it: ''Tisn't what you blanky *do* that matters, it's what you blanky *have* to do.' In other words, worry, not work, kills.

E2's gun did its best to knock the heart out of them all. She had to shift the wretched thing twice; once because the bolts that held it down were smashed (the wire hawser must have pretty well pulled it off its seat), and again because the hull beneath it leaked on pressure. She went down to make sure of it. But she drilled and tapped and adjusted, till in a short time the gun worked again and killed steamers as it should. Meanwhile, the whole boat leaked. All the plates under the old gun-position forward leaked; she leaked aft through damaged hydroplane guards, and on her way home they had to keep the water down by hand pumps while she was diving through the nets. Where she did not leak outside she leaked internally, tank leaking into tank, so that the petrol got into the main fresh-water supply and the men had to be put on allowance. The last pint was served out when she was in the narrowest part of the Narrows, a place where one's mouth may well go dry of a sudden.

Here for the moment the records end. I have been at some pains not to pick and choose among them. So far from doctoring or heightening any of the incidents, I have rather understated them; but I hope I have made it clear that through all the haste and fury of these multiplied actions, when life and death and destruction turned on the twitch of a finger, not one life of any non-combatant was wittingly taken. They were carefully picked up or picked out, taken below, transferred to boats, and despatched or personally conducted in the intervals of business to the safe, unexploding beach. Sometimes they part from their chaperones 'with many expressions of good will,' at others they seem greatly relieved and rather surprised at not being knocked on the head after the custom of their Allies. But the boats with a hundred things on their minds no more take credit for their humanity than their commanders explain the feats for which they won their respective decorations.

DESTROYERS AT JUTLAND

1916

'HAVE you news of my boy Jack?'
            Not this tide.
'When d'you think that he'll come back?'
            Not with this wind blowing, and this tide.

'Has any one else had word of him?'
            Not this tide.
For what is sunk will hardly swim,
            Not with this wind blowing and this tide.

'Oh, dear, what comfort can I find?'
            None this tide,
            Nor any tide,
Except he didn't shame his kind
            Not even with that wind blowing and
                        that tide.

Then hold your head up all the more,
            This tide,
            And every tide,
Because he was the son you bore,
            And gave to that wind blowing and that
                        tide!

STORIES OF THE BATTLE

CRIPPLE AND PARALYTIC

I

THERE was much destroyer-work in the Battle of Jutland. The actual battle field may not have been more than twenty thousand square miles, but the incidental patrols, from first to last, must have covered many times that area. Doubtless the next generation will comb out every detail of it. All we need remember is there were many squadrons of battleships and cruisers engaged over the face of the North Sea, and that they were accompanied in their dread comings and goings by multitudes of destroyers, who attacked the enemy both by day and by night from the afternoon of May 31 to the morning of June 1, 1916. We are too close to the gigantic canvas to take in the meaning of the picture; our children stepping backward through the years may get the true perspective and proportions.

To recapitulate what every one knows.

The German fleet came out of its North Sea ports, scouting

ships ahead; then destroyers, cruisers, battle-cruisers, and, last, the main battle fleet in the rear. It moved north, parallel with the coast of stolen Schleswig-Holstein and Jutland. Our fleets were already out; the main battle fleet (Admiral Jellicoe) sweeping down from the north, and our battle-cruiser fleet (Admiral Beatty) feeling for the enemy. Our scouts came in contact with the enemy on the afternoon of May 31 about 100 miles off the Jutland coast, steering north-west. They satisfied themselves he was in strength, and reported accordingly to our battle-cruiser fleet, which engaged the enemy's battle-cruisers at about half-past three o'clock. The enemy steered south-east to rejoin their own fleet, which was coming up from that quarter. We fought him on a parallel course as he ran for more than an hour.

Then his battle-fleet came in sight, and Beatty's fleet went about and steered north-west in order to retire on our battle-fleet, which was hurrying down from the north. We returned fighting very much over the same waters as we had used in our slant south. The enemy up till now had lain to the eastward of us, whereby he had the advantage in that thick weather of seeing our hulls clear against the afternoon light, while he himself worked in the mists. We then steered a little to the north-west bearing him off towards the east till at six o'clock Beatty had headed the enemy's leading ships and our main battle-fleet came in sight from the north. The enemy broke back in a loop, first eastward, then south, then south-west as our fleet edged him off from the land, and our main battle-fleet, coming up behind them, followed in their wake. Thus for a while we had the enemy to westward of us, where he made a better mark; but the day was closing and the weather thickened, and the enemy wanted to get away. At a quarter past eight the enemy, still heading south-west, was covered by his destroyers in a great screen of grey smoke, and he got away.

Night And Morning

As darkness fell, our fleets lay between the enemy and his home ports. During the night our heavy ships, keeping well clear of possible mine-fields, swept down south to south and west of the Horns Reef, so that they might pick him up in the morning. When morning came our main fleet could find no trace of the enemy to the southward, but our destroyer-flotillas further north had been very busy with enemy ships, apparently running for the Horns Reef Channel. It looks, then, as if when we lost sight of the enemy in the smoke screen and the darkness he had changed course and broken for home astern our main fleets. And whether that was a sound manoeuvre or otherwise, he and the still flows of the North Sea alone can tell.

But how is a layman to give any coherent account of an affair where a whole country's coast-line was background to battle covering geographical degrees? The records give an impression of illimitable grey waters, nicked on their uncertain horizons with the smudge and blur of ships sparkling with fury against ships hidden under the curve of the world. One sees these distances maddeningly obscured by walking mists and weak fogs, or wiped out by layers of funnel and gun smoke, and realises how, at the pace the ships were going, anything might be stumbled upon in the haze or charge out of it when it lifted. One comprehends, too, how the far-off glare of a great vessel afire might be reported as a local fire on a near-by enemy, or *vice versa*; how a silhouette caught, for an instant, in a shaft of pale light let down from the low sky might be fatally difficult to identify till too late. But add to all these inevitable confusions and misreckonings of time, shape, and distance, charges at every angle of squadrons through and across other squadrons; sudden shifts of the centres of the fights, and even swifter restorations; wheelings, sweepings, and regroupments such as accompany the passage across space of colliding universes. Then blanket the whole inferno with the darkness of night at full speed, and – see what you can make of it.

THREE DESTROYERS

A little time after the action began to heat up between our battle-cruisers and the enemy's, eight or ten of our destroyers opened the ball for their branch of the service by breaking up the attack of an enemy light cruiser and fifteen destroyers. Of these they accounted for at least two destroyers – some think more – and drove the others back on their battle-cruisers. This scattered that fight a good deal over the sea. Three of our destroyers held on for the enemy's battle-fleet, who came down on them at ranges which eventually grew less than 3000 yards. Our people ought to have been lifted off the seas bodily, but they managed to fire a couple of torpedoes apiece while the range was diminishing. They had no illusions. Says one of the three, speaking of her second shot, which she loosed at fairly close range, 'This torpedo was fired because it was considered very unlikely that the ship would escape disablement before another opportunity offered.' But still they lived – three destroyers against all a battle-cruiser fleet's quick-firers, as well as the fire of a batch of enemy destroyers at 600 yards. And they were thankful for small mercies. 'The position being favourable,' a third torpedo was fired from each while they yet floated.

At 2500 yards, one destroyer was hit somewhere in the vitals and swerved badly across her next astern, who 'was obliged to alter course to avoid a collision, thereby failing to fire a fourth torpedo.' Then that next astern 'observed signal for destroyers' recall,' and went back to report to her flotilla captain – alone. Of her two companions, one was 'badly hit and remained stopped between the lines.' The other 'remained stopped, but was afloat when last seen.' Ships that 'remain stopped' are liable to be rammed or sunk by methodical gun-fire. That was, perhaps, fifty minutes' work put in before there was any really vicious 'edge' to the action, and it did not steady the nerves of the enemy battle-cruisers any more than another attack made by another detachment of ours.

'What does one do when one passes a ship that 'remains stopped'?' I asked of a youth who had had experience.

'Nothing special. They cheer, and you cheer back. One doesn't think about it till afterwards. You see, it may be your luck in another minute.'

Luck

There were many other torpedo attacks in all parts of the battle that misty afternoon, including a quaint episode of an enemy light cruiser who 'looked as if she were trying' to torpedo one of our battle-cruisers while the latter was particularly engaged. A destroyer of ours, returning from a special job which required delicacy, was picking her way back at 30 knots through batches of enemy battle-cruisers and light cruisers with the idea of attaching herself to the nearest destroyer-flotilla and making herself useful. It occurred to her that as she 'was in a most advantageous position for repelling enemy's destroyers endeavouring to attack, she could not do better than to remain on the 'engaged bow' of our battle-cruiser.' So she remained and considered things.

There was an enemy battle-cruiser squadron in the offing; with several enemy light cruisers ahead of that squadron, and the weather was thickish and deceptive. She sighted the enemy light cruiser, 'class uncertain,' only a few thousand yards away, and 'decided to attack her in order to frustrate her firing torpedoes at our Battle Fleet.' (This in case the authorities should think that light cruiser wished to buy rubber.) So she fell upon the light cruiser with every gun she had, at between two and four thousand yards, and secured a number of hits, just the same as at target practice. While thus occupied she sighted out of the mist a squadron of enemy battle-cruisers that had worried her earlier in the afternoon. Leaving the light cruiser, she closed to what she considered a reasonable distance of the newcomers, and let them have, as she thought, both her torpedoes. She possessed an active Acting Sub-Lieutenant, who, though officers of that rank think otherwise, is not very far removed from an ordinary midshipman of the type one sees in tow of relatives at the Army and Navy Stores. He sat astride one of the tubes to make quite sure things were in order, and fired when the sights came on.

But, at that very moment, a big shell hit the destroyer on the side and there was a tremendous escape of steam. Believing – since she had seen one torpedo leave the tube before the smash came – believing that both her tubes had been fired, the destroyer turned away 'at greatly reduced speed' (the shell reduced it), and passed, quite reasonably close, the light cruiser whom she had been hammering so faithfully till the larger game appeared. Meantime, the Sub-Lieutenant was exploring what damage had been done by the big shell. He discovered that only *one* of the two torpedoes had left the tubes, and 'observing enemy light cruiser beam on and apparently temporarily stopped,' he fired the providential remainder at her, and it hit her below the conning-tower and well and truly exploded, as was witnessed by the Sub-Lieutenant himself, the Commander, a leading signalman, and several other ratings. Luck continued to hold! The Acting Sub-Lieutenant further reported that 'we still had three torpedoes left and at the same time drew my attention to enemy's line of battleships.' They rather looked as if they were coming down with intent to assault. So the Sub-Lieutenant fired the rest of the torpedoes, which at least started off correctly from the shell-shaken tubes, and must have crossed the enemy's line. When torpedoes turn up among a squadron, they upset the steering and distract the attention of all concerned. Then the destroyer judged it time to take stock of her injuries. Among other minor defects she could neither steam, steer, nor signal.

Towing Under Diffficulties

Mark how virtue is rewarded! Another of our destroyers an hour or so previously had been knocked clean out of action, before she had done anything, by a big shell which gutted a boiler-room and started an oil fire. (That is the drawback to oil.) She crawled out between the battleships till she 'reached an area of comparative calm' and repaired damage. She says: 'The fire having been dealt with, it was found a mat kept the stokehold dry. My only trouble now being lack of speed, I looked round for useful employment, and saw a destroyer in great difficulties, so closed her.' That destroyer was our paralytic friend of the intermittent torpedo-tubes, and a grateful ship she was when her crippled sister (but still good for a few knots) offered her a tow, 'under very trying conditions with large enemy ships approaching.' So the two set off together, Cripple and Paralytic, with heavy shells falling round them, as sociable as a couple of lame hounds. Cripple worked up to 12 knots, and the weather grew vile, and the tow parted. Paralytic, by this time, had raised steam in a boiler or two, and made shift to get along slowly on her own, Cripple hirpling beside her, till Paralytic could not make any more headway in that rising sea, and Cripple had to tow her once more. Once more the tow parted. So they tied Paralytic up rudely and effectively with a cable round her after bollards and gun (presumably because of strained forward bulkheads) and hauled her stern-first, through heavy seas, at continually reduced speeds, doubtful of their position, unable to sound because of the seas, and much pestered by a wind which backed without warning, till, at last, they made land, and turned into the hospital appointed for brave wounded ships. Everybody speaks well of Cripple. Her name crops up in several reports, with such compliments as the men of the sea use when they see good work. She herself speaks well of her Lieutenant, who, as executive officer, 'took charge of the fire and towing arrangements in a very creditable manner,' and also of Tom Battye and Thomas Kerr, engine-room artificer and stoker petty officer, who 'were in the stokehold at the time of the shell striking, and performed cool and prompt decisive action, although both suffering from shock and slight injuries.'

Useful Employment

Have you ever noticed that men who do Homeric deeds often describe them in Homeric language? The sentence 'I looked round for useful employment' is worthy of Ulysses when 'there was an evil sound at the ships of men who perished and of the ships themselves broken at the same time.'

Roughly, very roughly, speaking, our destroyers enjoyed three phases of 'prompt decisive action' – the first, a period of daylight attacks (from 4 to 6 P.M.) such as the one I have just described, while the battle was young and the light fairly good on the afternoon of May 31; the second, towards dark, when the light had lessened and the enemy were more uneasy, and, I think, in more scattered formation; the third, when darkness had fallen, and the destroyers had been strung out astern with orders to help the enemy home, which they did all night as opportunity offered. One cannot say whether the day or the night work was the more desperate. From private advices, the young gentlemen concerned seem to have functioned with efficiency either way. As one of them said: 'After a bit, you see, we were all pretty much on our own, and you could really find out what your ship could do.'

I will tell you later of a piece of night work not without merit.

The Night Hunt

Ramming An Enemy Cruiser

II

As I said, we will confine ourselves to something quite sane and simple which does not involve more than half-a-dozen different reports.

When the German fleet ran for home, on the night of May 31, it seems to have scattered – 'starred,' I believe, is the word for the evolution – in a general *sauve qui peut*, while the Devil, livelily represented by our destroyers, took the hindmost. Our flotillas were strung out far and wide on this job. One man compared it to hounds hunting half a hundred separate foxes.

I take the adventures of several couples of destroyers who, on the night of May 31, were nosing along somewhere towards the Schleswig-Holstein coast, ready to chop any Hun-stuff coming back to earth by that particular road. The leader of one line was Gehenna, and the next two ships astern of her were Eblis and Shaitan, in the order given. There were others, of course, but with the exception of one Goblin they don't come violently into this tale. There had been a good deal of promiscuous firing that evening, and actions were going on all round. Towards midnight our destroyers were overtaken by several three-and four-funnel German ships (cruisers they thought) hurrying home. At this stage of the game anybody might have been anybody – pursuer or pursued. The Germans took no chances, but switched on their searchlights and opened fire on Gehenna. Her acting sub-lieutenant reports: 'A salvo hit us forward. I opened fire with the after-guns. A shell then struck us in a steam-pipe, and I could see nothing but steam. But both starboard torpedo-tubes were fired.'

Eblis, Gehenna's next astern, at once fired a torpedo at the second ship in the German line, a four-funnelled cruiser, and hit her between the second funnel and the mainmast, when 'she appeared to catch fire fore and aft simultaneously, heeled right over to starboard, and undoubtedly sank.' Eblis loosed off a second torpedo and turned aside to reload, firing at the same time to distract the enemy's attention from Gehenna, who was now ablaze fore and aft. Gehenna's acting sub-lieutenant (the only executive officer who survived) says that by the time the steam from the broken pipe cleared he found Gehenna stopped, nearly everybody amidships killed or wounded, the cartridge-boxes round the guns exploding one after the other as the fires took hold, and the enemy not to be seen. Three minutes or less did all that damage. Eblis had nearly finished reloading when a shot struck the davit that was swinging her last torpedo into the tube and wounded all hands concerned.

Thereupon she dropped torpedo work, fired at an enemy searchlight which winked and went out, and was closing in to help Gehenna when she found herself under the noses of a couple of enemy cruisers. 'The nearer one,' he says, 'altered course to ram me apparently.' The Senior Service writes in curiously lawyer-like fashion, but there is no denying that they act quite directly. 'I therefore put my helm hard aport and the two ships met and rammed each other, port bow to port bow.' There could have been no time to think and, for Eblis's commander on the bridge, none to gather information. But he had observant subordinates, and he writes – and I would humbly suggest that the words be made the ship's motto for evermore – he writes, 'Those aft noted' that the enemy cruiser had certain marks on her funnel and certain arrangements of derricks on each side which, quite apart from the evidence she left behind her, betrayed her class. Eblis and she met. Says Eblis: 'I consider I must have considerably damaged this cruiser, as 20 feet of her side plating was left in my foc'sle.' Twenty feet of ragged rivet-slinging steel, razoring and reaping about in the dark on a foc'sle that had collapsed like a concertina! It was very fair plating too. There were side-scuttle holes in it – what we passengers would call portholes. But it might have been better, for Eblis reports sorrowfully, 'by the thickness of the coats of paint (duly given in 32nds of the inch) she would not appear to have been a very new ship.'

New or old, the enemy had done her best. She had completely demolished Eblis's bridge and searchlight platform, brought down the mast and the fore-funnel, ruined the whaler and the dinghy, split the foc'sle open above water from the stem to the galley which is abaft the bridge, and below water had opened it up from the stem to the second bulkhead. She had further ripped off Eblis's skin-plating for an amazing number of yards on one side of her, and had fired a couple of large-calibre shells into Eblis at point-blank range, narrowly missing her vitals. Even so, Eblis is as impartial as a prize-court. She reports that the second shot, a trifle of eight inches, 'may have been fired at a different time or just after colliding.' But the night was yet young, and 'just after getting clear of this cruiser an enemy battle-cruiser grazed past our stern at high speed' and again the judgmatic mind – 'I think she must have intended to ram us.' She was a large three-funnelled thing, her centre funnel shot away and 'lights were flickering under her foc'sle as if she was on fire forward.' Fancy the vision of her, hurtling out of the dark, red-lighted from within, and fleeing on like a man with his throat cut!

As an interlude, all enemy cruisers that night were not keen on ramming. They wanted to get home. A man I know who was on another part of the drive saw a covey bolt through our destroyers; and had just settled himself for a shot at one of them when the night threw up a second bird coming down full speed on his other beam. He had bare time to jink between

117

the two as they whizzed past. One switched on her searchlight and fired a whole salvo at him point blank. The heavy stuff went between his funnels. She must have sighted along her own beam of light, which was about a thousand yards.

'How did you feel?' I asked.

'I was rather sick. It was my best chance all that night, and I had to miss it or be cut in two.'

'What happened to the cruisers?'

'Oh, they went on, and I heard 'em being attended to by some of our fellows. They didn't know what they were doing, or they couldn't have missed me sitting, the way they did.'

The Confidential Books

After all that Eblis picked herself up, and discovered that she was still alive, with a dog's chance of getting to port. But she did not bank on it. That grand slam had wrecked the bridge, pinning the commander under the wreckage. By the time he had extricated himself he 'considered it advisable to throw overboard the steel chest and dispatch-box of confidential and secret books.' These are never allowed to fall into strange hands, and their proper disposal is the last step but one in the ritual of the burial service of His Majesty's ships at sea. Gehenna, afire and sinking, out somewhere in the dark, was going through it on her own account. This is her Acting Sub-Lieutenant's report: 'The confidential books were got up. The First Lieutenant gave the order: 'Every man aft,' and the confidential books were thrown overboard. The ship soon afterwards heeled over to starboard and the bows went under. The First Lieutenant gave the order: 'Everybody for themselves.' The ship sank in about a minute, the stern going straight up into the air.'

But it was not written in the Book of Fate that stripped and battered Eblis should die that night as Gehenna died. After the burial of the books it was found that the several fires on her were manageable, that she 'was not making water aft of the damage,' which meant two-thirds of her were, more or less, in commission, and, best of all, that three boilers were usable in spite of the cruiser's shells. So she 'shaped course and speed to make the least water and the most progress towards land.' On the way back the wind shifted eight points without warning – it was this shift, if you remember, that so embarrassed Cripple and Paralytic on their homeward crawl – and, what with one thing and another, Eblis was unable to make port till the scandalously late hour of noon on June 2, 'the mutual ramming having occurred about 11.40 P.M. on May 31.' She says, this time without any legal reservation whatever, 'I cannot speak too highly of the courage, discipline, and devotion of the officers and ship's company.'

Her recommendations are a Compendium of Godly Deeds for the Use of Mariners. They cover pretty much all that man may be expected to do. There was, as there always is, a first lieutenant who, while his commander was being extricated from the bridge wreckage, took charge of affairs and steered the ship first from the engine-room, or what remained of it, and later from aft, and otherwise manoeuvred as requisite, among doubtful bulkheads. In his leisure he 'improvised means of signalling,' and if there be not one joyous story behind that smooth sentence I am a Hun!

The Art Of Improvising

They all improvised like the masters of craft they were. The chief engine-room artificer, after he had helped to put out fires, improvised stops to the gaps which were left by the carrying away of the forward funnel and mast. He got and kept up steam 'to a much higher point than would have appeared at all possible,' and when the sea rose, as it always does if you are in trouble, he 'improvised pumping and drainage arrangements, thus allowing the ship to steam at a good speed on the whole.' There could not have been more than 40 feet of hole.

The surgeon – probationer – performed an amputation single-handed in the wreckage by the bridge, and by his 'wonderful skill, resource, and unceasing care and devotion undoubtedly saved the lives of the many seriously wounded men.' That no horror might be lacking, there was 'a short circuit among the bridge wreckage for a considerable time.' The searchlight and wireless were tangled up together, and the electricity leaked into everything.

There were also three wise men who saved the ship whose names must not be forgotten. They were Chief Engine-room Artificer Lee, Stoker Petty Officer Gardiner, and Stoker Elvins.

When the funnel carried away it was touch and go whether the foremost boiler would not explode. These three 'put on respirators and kept the fans going till all fumes, etc., were cleared away.' To each man, you will observe, his own particular Hell which he entered of his own particular initiative.

Lastly, there were the two remaining Quartermasters – mutinous dogs, both of 'em – one wounded in the right hand and the other in the left, who took the wheel between them all the way home, thus improvising one complete Navy-pattern Quartermaster, and 'refused to be relieved during the whole thirty-six hours before the ship returned to port.' So Eblis passes out of the picture with 'never a moan or complaint from a single wounded man, and in spite of the rough weather of June 1 they all remained cheery.' They had one Hun cruiser, torpedoed, to their credit, and strong evidence abroad that they had knocked the end out of another.

But Gehenna went down, and those of her crew who remained hung on to the rafts that destroyers carry till they were picked up about the dawn by Shaitan, third in the line, who, at that hour, was in no shape to give much help. Here is Shaitan's tale. She saw the unknown cruisers overtake the flotilla, saw their leader switch on searchlights and open fire as she drew abreast of Gehenna, and at once fired a torpedo at the third German ship. Shaitan could not see Eblis, her next ahead, for, as we know, Eblis after firing her torpedoes had hauled off to reload. When the enemy switched his searchlights off Shaitan hauled out too. It is not wholesome for destroyers to keep on the same course within a thousand yards of big enemy cruisers.

She picked up a destroyer of another division, Goblin, who for the moment had not been caught by the enemy's searchlights and had profited by this decent obscurity to fire a torpedo at the hindmost of the cruisers. Almost as Shaitan took station behind Goblin the latter was lighted up by a large ship and heavily fired at. The enemy fled, but she left Goblin out of control, with a grisly list of casualties, and her helm jammed. Goblin swerved, returned, and swerved again; Shaitan astern tried to clear her, and the two fell aboard each other, Goblin's bows deep in Shaitan's fore-bridge. While they hung thus, locked, an unknown destroyer rammed Shaitan aft, cutting off several feet of her stern and leaving her rudder jammed hard over. As complete a mess as the Personal Devil himself could have devised, and all due to the merest accident of a few panicky salvoes. Presently the two ships worked clear in a smother of steam and oil, and went their several ways. Quite a while after she had parted from Shaitan, Goblin discovered several of Shaitan's people, some of them wounded, on her own foc'sle, where they had been pitched by the collision. Goblin, working her way homeward on such boilers as remained, carried on a one-gun fight at a few cables' distance with some enemy destroyers, who, not knowing what state she was in, sheered off after a few rounds. Shaitan, holed forward and opened up aft, came across the survivors from Gehenna clinging to their raft, and took them aboard. Then some of our destroyers – they were thick on the sea that night – tried to tow her stern-first, for Goblin had cut her up badly forward. But, since Shaitan lacked any stern, and her rudder was jammed hard across where the stern should have been, the hawsers parted, and, after leave asked of lawful authority, across all that waste of waters, they sank Shaitan by gun-fire, having first taken all the proper steps about the confidential books. Yet Shaitan had had her little crumb of comfort ere the end. While she lay crippled she saw quite close to her a German cruiser that was trailing homeward in the dawn gradually heel over and sink.

This completes my version of the various accounts of the four destroyers directly concerned for a few hours, on one minute section of one wing of our battle. Other ships witnessed other aspects of the agony and duly noted them as they went about their business. One of our battleships, for instance, made out by the glare of burning Gehenna that the supposed cruiser that Eblis torpedoed was a German battleship of a certain class. So Gehenna did not die in vain, and we may take it that the discovery did not unduly depress Eblis's wounded in hospital.

ASKING FOR TROUBLE *

The rest of the flotilla that the four destroyers belonged to had their own adventures later. One of them, chasing or being chased, saw Goblin out of control just before Goblin and Shaitan locked, and narrowly escaped adding herself to that triple collision. Another loosed a couple of torpedoes at the enemy ships who were attacking Gehenna, which, perhaps, accounts for the anxiety of the enemy to break away from that hornets' nest as soon as possible. Half a dozen or so of them ran into four German battleships, which they set about torpedoing at ranges varying from half a mile to a mile and a half. It was asking for trouble and they got it; but they got in return at least one big ship, and the same observant battleship of ours who identified Eblis's bird reported *three* satisfactory explosions in half an hour, followed by a glare that lit up all the sky. One of the flotilla, closing on what she thought was the smoke of a sister in difficulties, found herself well in among the four battleships. 'It was too late to get away,' she says, so she attacked, fired her torpedo, was caught up in the glare of a couple of searchlights, and pounded to pieces in five minutes, not even her rafts being left. She went down with her colours flying, having fought to the last available gun. Another destroyer who had borne a hand in Gehenna's trouble had her try at the four battleships and got in a torpedo at 800 yards. She saw it explode and the ship take a heavy list. 'Then I was chased,' which is not surprising. She picked up a friend who could only do 20 knots. They sighted several Hun destroyers who fled from them; then dropped on to four Hun destroyers all together, who made great parade of commencing action, but soon afterwards 'thought better of it, and turned away.' So you see, in that flotilla alone there was every variety of fight, from the ordered attacks of squadrons under control, to single ship affairs, every turn of which depended on the second's decision of the men concerned; endurance to the hopeless end; bluff and cunning; reckless advance and red-hot flight; clear vision and as much of blank bewilderment as the Senior Service permits its children to indulge in. That is not much. When a destroyer who has been dodging enemy torpedoes and gun-fire in the dark realises about midnight that she is 'following a strange British flotilla, having lost sight of my own,' she 'decides to remain with them,' and shares their fortunes and whatever language is going.

If lost hounds could speak when they cast up next day, after an unchecked night among the wild life of the dark, they would talk much as our destroyers do.

The doorkeepers of Zion,
  They do not always stand
In helmet and whole armour,
  With halberds in their hand;
But, being sure of Zion,
  And all her mysteries,
They rest awhile in Zion,
Sit down and smile in Zion;
Ay, even jest in Zion,
  In Zion, at their ease.

The gatekeepers of Baal,
  They dare not sit or lean,
But fume and fret and posture
  And foam and curse between;
For being bound to Baal,
  Whose sacrifice is vain,
Their rest is scant with Baal,
They glare and pant for Baal,

They mouth and rant for Baal,
  For Baal in their pain.

But we will go to Zion,
  By choice and not through dread,
With these our present comrades
  And those our present dead;
And, being free of Zion
  In both her fellowships,
Sit down and sup in Zion –
Stand up and drink in Zion
Whatever cup in Zion
  Is offered to our lips!

THE MEANING OF 'JOSS'

III

A S one digs deeper into the records, one sees the various temperaments of men revealing themselves through all the formal wording. One commander may be an expert in torpedo-work, whose first care is how and where his shots went, and whether, under all circumstances of pace, light, and angle, the best had been achieved. Destroyers do not carry unlimited stocks of torpedoes. It rests with commanders whether they shall spend with a free hand at first or save for night-work ahead – risk a possible while he is yet afloat, or hang on coldly for a certainty. So in the old whaling days did the harponeer bring up or back off his boat till some shift of the great fish's bulk gave him sure opening at the deep-seated life.

And then comes the question of private judgment. 'I thought so-and-so would happen. Therefore, I did thus and thus.' Things may or may not turn out as anticipated, but that is merely another of the million chances of the sea. Take a case in point. A flotilla of our destroyers sighted six (there had been eight the previous afternoon) German battleships of Kingly and Imperial caste very early in the morning of the June 1, and duly attacked. At first our people ran parallel to the enemy, then, as far as one can make out, headed them and swept round sharp to the left, firing torpedoes from their port or left-hand tubes. Between them they hit a battleship, which went up in flame and *débris*. But one of the flotilla had not turned with the rest. She had anticipated that the attack would be made on another quarter, and, for certain technical reasons, she was not ready. When she was, she turned, and single-handed – the rest of the flotilla having finished and gone on – carried out two attacks on the five remaining battleships. She got one of them amidships, causing a terrific explosion and flame above the masthead, which signifies that the magazine has been touched off. She counted the battleships when the smoke had cleared, and there were but four of them. She herself was not hit, though shots fell close. She went her way, and, seeing nothing of her sisters, picked up another flotilla and stayed with it till the end. Do I make clear the maze of blind hazard and wary judgment in which our men of the sea must move?

Saved By A Smoke Screen

Some of the original flotilla were chased and headed about by cruisers after their attack on the six battleships, and a single shell from battleship or cruiser reduced one of them to such a condition that she was brought home by her sub-lieutenant and a midshipman. Her captain, first lieutenant, gunner, torpedo coxswain, and both signalmen were either killed or wounded; the bridge, with charts, instruments, and signalling gear went; all torpedoes were expended; a gun was out of action, and the usual cordite fires developed. Luckily, the engines were workable. She escaped under cover of a smoke-screen, which is an unbearably filthy outpouring of the densest smoke, made by increasing the proportion of oil to air in the furnace-feed. It rolls forth from the funnels looking solid enough to sit upon, spreads in a searchlight-proof pat of impenetrable beastliness, and in still weather hangs for hours. But it saved that ship.

It is curious to note the subdued tone of a boy's report when by some accident of slaughter he is raised to command. There are certain formalities which every ship must comply with on entering certain ports. No fully-striped commander would trouble to detail them any more than he would the aspect of his Club porter. The young 'un puts it all down, as who should say: 'I rang the bell, wiped my feet on the mat, and asked if they were at home.' He is most careful of the port proprieties, and since he will be sub. again tomorrow, and all his equals will tell him exactly how he ought to have handled her, he almost apologises for the steps he took – deeds which ashore might be called cool or daring.

The Senior Service does not gush. There are certain formulae appropriate to every occasion. One of our destroyers, who was knocked out early in the day and lay helpless, was sighted by several of her companions. One of them reported her to the authorities, but, being busy at the time, said he did not think himself justified in hampering himself with a disabled ship in the middle of an action. It was not as if she was sinking either. She was only holed foreward and aft, with a bad hit in the engine-room, and her steering-gear knocked out. In this posture she cheered the passing ships, and set about repairing her hurts with good heart and a smiling countenance. She managed to get under some sort of way at midnight, and next day was taken in tow by a friend. She says officially, 'his assistance was invaluable, as I had no oil left and met heavy weather.'

What actually happened was much less formal. Fleet destroyers, as a rule, do not worry about navigation. They take their orders from the flagship, and range out and return, on signal, like sheep-dogs whose fixed point is their shepherd. Consequently, when they break loose on their own they may fetch up rather doubtful of their whereabouts – as this injured one did. After she had been so kindly taken in tow, she inquired of her friend ('Message captain to captain') – 'Have you any notion where we are?' The friend replied, 'I have not, but I will find out.' So the friend waited on the sun with the necessary implements, which luckily had not been smashed, and in due time made: 'Our observed position at this hour is thus and thus.' The tow, irreverently, 'Is it? Didn't know you were a navigator.' The friend, with hauteur, 'Yes; it's rather a hobby of mine.' The tow, 'Had no idea it was as bad as all that; but I'm afraid I'll have to trust you this time. Go ahead, and be quick about it.' They reached a port, correctly enough, but to this hour the tow, having studied with the friend at a place called Dartmouth, insists that it was pure Joss.

And Joss, which is luck, fortune, destiny, the irony of Fate or Nemesis, is the greatest of all the Battle-gods that move on the waters. As I will show you later, knowledge of gunnery and a delicate instinct for what is in the enemy's minds may enable a destroyer to thread her way, slowing, speeding, and twisting between the heavy salvoes of opposing fleets. As the dank-smelling waterspouts rise and break, she judges where the next grove of them will sprout. If her judgment is correct, she may enter it in her report as a little feather in her cap. But it is Joss when the stray 12-inch shell, hurled by a giant at some giant ten miles away, falls on her from Heaven and wipes out her and her profound calculations. This was seen to happen to a Hun destroyer in mid-attack. While she was being laboriously dealt with by a 4-inch gun something immense took her, and – she was not.

Joss it is, too, when the cruiser's 8-inch shot, that should have raked out your innards from the forward boiler to the ward-room stove, deflects miraculously, like a twig dragged through deep water, and, almost returning on its track, skips off unbursten and leaves you reprieved by the breadth of a nail from three deaths in one. Later, a single splinter, no more, may cut your oil-supply pipes as dreadfully and completely as a broken wind-screen in a collision cuts the surprised motorist's throat. Then you must lie useless, fighting oil-fires while the precious fuel gutters away till you have to ask leave to escape while there are yet a few tons left. One ship who was once bled white by such a piece of Joss, suggested it would be better that oil-pipes should be led along certain lines which she sketched. As if that would make any difference to Joss when he wants to show what he can do!

Our sea-people, who have worked with him for a thousand wettish years, have acquired something of Joss's large toleration and humour. He causes ships in thick weather, or under strain, to mistake friends for enemies. At such times, if your heart is full of highly organized hate, you strafe frightfully and efficiently till one of you perishes, and the survivor reports wonders which are duly wirelessed all over the world. But if you worship Joss, you reflect, you put two and two together in a casual insular way, and arrive – sometimes both parties arrive – at instinctive conclusions which avoid trouble.

AN AFFAIR IN THE NORTH SEA

Witness this tale. It does not concern the Jutland fight, but another little affair which took place a while ago in the North Sea. It was understood that a certain type of cruiser of ours would *not* be taking part in a certain show. Therefore, if anyone saw cruisers very like them he might blaze at them with a clear conscience, for they would be Hun-boats. And one of our destroyers – thick weather as usual – spied the silhouettes of cruisers exactly like our own stealing across the haze. Said the Commander to his Sub., with an inflection neither period, exclamation, nor interrogation-mark can render – 'That – is – them.'

Said the Sub. in precisely the same tone – 'That is them, sir.'

'As my Sub.,' said the Commander, 'your observation is strictly in accord with the traditions of the Service. Now, as man to man, what *are* they?' 'We-el,' said the Sub., 'since you put it that way, I'm d----d if *I'd* fire.' And they didn't, and they were quite right. The destroyer had been off on another job, and Joss had jammed the latest wireless orders to her at the last moment. But Joss had also put it into the hearts of the boys to save themselves and others.

I hold no brief for the Hun, but honestly I think he has not lied as much about the Jutland fight as people believe, and that when he protests he sank a ship, he *did* very completely sink a ship. I am the more confirmed in this belief by a still small voice among the Jutland reports, musing aloud over an account of an unaccountable outlying brawl witnessed by one of our destroyers. The voice suggests that what the destroyer saw was one German ship being sunk by another. Amen!

Our destroyers saw a good deal that night on the face of the waters. Some of them who were working in 'areas of comparative calm' submit charts of their tangled courses, all studded with notes along the zigzag – something like this: –

8 P.M. – *Heard explosion to the N.W.* (A neat arrow-head points that way.) Half an inch farther along, a short change of course, and the word *Hit* explains the meaning of – '*Sighted enemy cruiser engaged with destroyers.*' Another twist follows. '9.30 P.M. – *Passed wreckage. Engaged enemy destroyers port beam opposite courses.*' A long straight line without incident, then a tangle, and – *Picked up survivors So-and-So.* A stretch over to some ship that they were transferred to, a fresh departure, and another brush

with '*Single destroyer on parallel course. Hit. 0.7 A.M. – Passed bows enemy cruiser sticking up. 0.18. – Joined flotilla for attack on battleship squadron.*' So it runs on – one little ship in a few short hours passing through more wonders of peril and accident than all the old fleets ever dreamed.

A 'CHILD'S' LETTER

In years to come naval experts will collate all those diagrams, and furiously argue over them. A lot of the destroyer work was inevitably as mixed as bombing down a trench, as the scuffle of a polo match, or as the hot heaving heart of a football scrum. It is difficult to realise when one considers the size of the sea, that it is that very size and absence of boundary which helps the confusion. To give an idea, here is a letter (it has been quoted before, I believe, but it is good enough to repeat many times), from a nineteen-year-old child to his friend aged seventeen (and minus one leg), in a hospital:

'I'm so awfully sorry you weren't in it. It was rather terrible, but a wonderful experience, and I wouldn't have missed it for anything, but, by Jove, it isn't a thing one wants to make a habit of.

'I must say it is very different from what I expected. I expected to be excited, but was not a bit. It's hard to express what we did feel like, but you know the sort of feeling one has when one goes in to bat at cricket, and rather a lot depends upon your doing well, and you are waiting for the first ball.

Well, it's very much the same as that. Do you know what I mean? A sort of tense feeling, not quite knowing what to expect. One does not feel the slightest bit frightened, and the idea that there's a chance of you and your ship being scuppered does not enter one's head. There are too many other things to think about.'

Follows the usual 'No ship like our ship' talkee, and a note of where she was at the time.

'Then they ordered us to attack, so we bustled off full bore. Being navigator, also having control of all the guns, I was on the bridge all the time, and remained for twelve hours without leaving it at all. When we got fairly close I sighted a good-looking Hun destroyer, which I thought I'd like to strafe. You know, it's awful fun to know that you can blaze off at a real ship, and do as much damage as you like. Well, I'd just got their range on the guns, and we'd just fired one round, when some more of our destroyers coming from the opposite direction got between us and the enemy and completely blanketed us, so we had to stop, which was rather rot. Shortly afterwards they recalled us, so we bustled back again. How any destroyer got out of it is perfectly wonderful.

'Literally there were hundreds of progs (shells falling) all round us, from a 15-in to a 4-in, and you know what a big splash a 15-in bursting in the water does make. We got washed through by the spray. Just as we were getting back, a whole salvo of big shells fell just in front of us and short of our big ships. The skipper and I did rapid calculations as to how long it would take them to reload, fire again, time of flight, etc., as we had to go right through the spot. We came to the conclusion that, as they were short a bit, they would probably go up a bit, and they didn't, but luckily they altered deflection, and the next fell right astern of us. Anyhow, we managed to come out of that row without the ship or a man on board being touched.

WHAT THE BIG SHIPS STAND

'It's extraordinary the amount of knocking about the big ships can stand. One saw them hit, and they seemed to be one mass of flame and smoke, and you think they're gone, but when the smoke clears away they are apparently none the worse and still firing away. But to see a ship blow up is a terrible and wonderful sight; an enormous volume of flame and smoke almost 200 feet high and great pieces of metal, etc., blown sky-high, and then when the smoke clears not a sign of the ship. We saw one other extraordinary sight. Of course, you know the North Sea is very shallow. We came across a Hun cruiser absolutely on end, his stern on the bottom and his bow sticking up about 30 feet in the water; and a little farther on a destroyer in precisely the same position.

'I couldn't be certain, but I rather think I saw your old ship crashing along and blazing away, but I expect you have heard from some of your pals. But the night was far and away the worse time of all. It was pitch dark, and, of course, absolutely no lights, and the firing seems so much more at night, as you could see the flashes lighting up the sky, and it seemed to make much more noise, and you could see ships on fire and blowing up. Of course *we* showed absolutely no lights. One expected to be surprised any moment, and eventually we were. We suddenly found ourselves within 1000 yards of two or three big Hun cruisers. They switched on their searchlights and started firing like nothing on earth. Then they put their searchlights on us, but for some extraordinary reason did not fire on us. As, of course, we were going full speed we lost them in a moment, but I must say, that I, and I think everybody else, thought that that was the end, but one does not feel afraid or panicky. I think I felt rather cooler then than at any other time. I asked lots of people afterwards what they felt like, and they all said the same thing. It all happens in a few seconds; one hasn't time to think; but never in all my life have I been so thankful to see daylight again – and I don't think I ever want to see another night like that – it's such an awful strain. One does not notice it at the time, but it's the reaction afterwards.

'I never noticed I was tired till I got back to harbour, and then we all turned in and absolutely slept like logs. We were seventy-two hours with little or no sleep. The skipper was perfectly wonderful. He never left the bridge for a minute for twenty-four hours, and was on the bridge or in the chart-house the whole time we were out (the chart-house is an airy dog-kennel that opens off the bridge) and I've never seen anybody so cool and unruffled. He stood there smoking his pipe as if nothing out of the ordinary were happening.

'One quite forgot all about time. I was relieved at 4 A.M., and on looking at my watch found I had been up there nearly twelve hours, and then discovered I was rather hungry. The skipper and I had some cheese and biscuits, ham sandwiches, and water on the bridge, and then I went down and brewed some cocoa and ship's biscuit.'

Not in the thick of the fight,
    Not in the press of the odds,
Do the heroes come to their height
    Or we know the demi-gods.

That stands over till peace.
    We can only perceive
Men returned from the seas,
    Very grateful for leave.

They grant us sudden days
    Snatched from their business of war.
We are too close to appraise
    What manner of men they are.

And whether their names go down
    With age-kept victories,
Or whether they battle and drown
    Unreckoned is hid from our eyes.

They are too near to be great,
　　　But our children shall understand
When and how our fate
　　　Was changed, and by whose hand.

Our children shall measure their worth.
　　　We are content to be blind,
For we know that we walk on a new-born earth
　　　With the saviours of mankind.

The Minds Of Men

How It Is Done

IV

WHAT mystery is there like the mystery of the other man's job – or what world so cut off as that which he enters when he goes to it? The eminent surgeon is altogether such an one as ourselves, even till his hand falls on the knob of the theatre door. After that, in the silence, among the ether fumes, no man except his acolytes, and they won't tell, has ever seen his face. So with the unconsidered curate. Yet, before the war, he had more experience of the business and detail of death than any of the people who contemned him. His face also, as he stands his bedside-watches – that countenance with which he shall justify himself to his Maker – none have ever looked upon. Even the ditcher is a priest of mysteries at the high moment when he lays out in his mind his levels and the fall of the water that he alone can draw off clearly. But catch any of these men five minutes after they have left their altars, and you will find the doors are shut.

Chance sent me almost immediately after the Jutland fight a Lieutenant of one of the destroyers engaged. Among other matters, I asked him if there was any particular noise.

'Well, I haven't been in the trenches, of course,' he replied, 'but I don't think there could have been much more noise than there was.'

This bears out a report of a destroyer who could not be certain whether an enemy battleship had blown up or not, saying that, in that particular corner, it would have been impossible to identify anything less than the explosion of a whole magazine.

'It wasn't exactly noise,' he reflected. 'Noise is what you take in from outside. This was *inside* you. It seemed to lift you right out of everything.'

'And how did the light affect one?' I asked, trying to work out a theory that noise and light produced beyond known endurance form an unknown anaesthetic and stimulant, comparable to, but infinitely more potent than, the soothing effect of the smoke-pall of ancient battles.

'The lights were rather curious,' was the answer. 'I don't know that one noticed searchlights particularly, unless they meant business; but when a lot of big guns loosed off together, the whole sea was lit up and you could see our destroyers running about like cockroaches on a tin soup-plate.'

'Then is black the best colour for our destroyers? Some commanders seem to think we ought to use grey.'

'Blessed if *I* know,' said young Dante. 'Everything shows black in that light. Then it all goes out again with a bang. Trying for the eyes if you are spotting.'

'And how did the dogs take it?' I pursued. There are several destroyers more or less owned by pet dogs, who start life as the chance-found property of a stoker, and end in supreme command of the bridge.

'Most of 'em didn't like it a bit. They went below one time, and wanted to be loved. They knew it wasn't ordinary practice.'

'What did Arabella do?' I had heard a good deal of Arabella.

'Oh, Arabella's *quite* different. Her job has always been to look after her master's pyjamas – folded up at the head of the bunk, you know. She found out pretty soon the bridge was no place for a lady, so she hopped downstairs and got in. You know how she makes three little jumps to it – first, on to the chair; then on the flap-table, and then up on the pillow. When the show was over, there she was as usual.'

'Was she glad to see her master?'

'*Ra-ather.* Arabella was the bold, gay lady-dog *then*!'

Now Arabella is between nine and eleven and a half inches long.

'Does the Hun run to pets at all?'

'I shouldn't say so. He's an unsympathetic felon – the Hun. But he might cherish a dachshund or so. We never picked up any ships' pets off him, and I'm sure we should if there had been.'

That I believed as implicitly as the tale of a destroyer attack some months ago, the object of which was to flush Zeppelins. It succeeded, for the flotilla was attacked by several. Right in the middle of the flurry, a destroyer asked permission to stop and lower dinghy to pick up ship's dog which had fallen overboard. Permission was granted, and the dog was duly rescued. 'Lord knows what the Hun made of it,' said my informant. 'He was rumbling round, dropping bombs; and the dinghy was digging out for all she was worth, and the Dog-Fiend was swimming for Dunkirk. It must have looked rather mad from above. But they saved the Dog-Fiend, and then everybody swore he was a German spy in disguise.'

The Fight

'And – about this Jutland fight?' I hinted, not for the first time.

'Oh, that was just a fight. There was more of it than any other fight, I suppose, but I expect all modern naval actions must be pretty much the same.'

'But what does one *do* – how does one feel?' I insisted, though I knew it was hopeless.

'One does one's job. Things are happening all the time. A man may be right under your nose one minute – serving a gun or something – and the next minute he isn't there.'

'And one notices that at the time?'

'Yes. But there's no time to keep *on* noticing it. You've got to carry on somehow or other, or your show stops. I tell you what one *does* notice, though. If one goes below for anything, or has to pass through a flat somewhere, and one sees the old wardroom clock ticking, or a photograph pinned up, or anything of that sort, one notices *that*. Oh yes, and there was another thing – the way a ship seemed to blow up if you were far off her. You'd see a glare, then a blaze, and then the smoke – miles high, lifting quite slowly. Then you'd get the row and the jar of it – just like bumping over submarines. Then, a long while after p'raps, you run through a regular rain of bits of burnt paper coming down on the decks – like showers of volcanic ash, you know.' The door of the operating-room seemed just about to open, but it shut again.

'And the Huns' gunnery?'

'That was various. Sometimes they began quite well, and went to pieces after they'd been strafed a little; but sometimes they picked up again. There was one Hun-boat that got no end of a hammering, and it seemed to do her gunnery good. She improved tremendously till we sank her. I expect we'd knocked out some scientific Hun in the controls, and he'd been succeeded by a man who knew how.'

It used to be 'Fritz' last year when they spoke of the enemy. Now it is Hun or, as I have heard, 'Yahun,' being a superlative of Yahoo. In the Napoleonic wars we called the Frenchmen too many names for any one of them to endure; but this is the age of standardisation.

'And what about our Lower Deck?' I continued.

'They? Oh, they carried on as usual. It takes a lot to impress the Lower Deck when they're busy.' And he mentioned several little things that confirmed this. They had a great deal to do, and they did it serenely because they had been trained to carry on under all conditions without panicking. What they did in the way of running repairs was even more wonderful, if that be possible, than their normal routine.

The Lower Deck nowadays is full of strange fish with unlooked-for accomplishments, as in the recorded case of two simple seamen of a destroyer who, when need was sorest, came to the front as trained experts in first-aid.

'And now – what about the actual Hun losses at Jutland?' I ventured.

'You've seen the list, haven't you?'

'Yes, but it occurred to me – that they might have been a shade under-estimated, and I thought perhaps –'

A perfectly plain asbestos fire-curtain descended in front of the already locked door. It was none of his business to dispute the drive. If there were any discrepancies between estimate and results, one might be sure that the enemy knew about them, which was the chief thing that mattered.

It was, said he, Joss that the light was so bad at the hour of the last round-up when our main fleet had come down from the north and shovelled the Hun round on his tracks. *Per contra*, had it been any other kind of weather, the odds were the Hun would not have ventured so far. As it was, the Hun's fleet had come out and gone back again, none the better for air and exercise. We must be thankful for what we had managed to pick up. But talking of picking up, there was an instance of almost unparalleled Joss which had stuck in his memory. A soldier-man, related to one of the officers in one of our ships that was put down, had got five days' leave from the trenches

147

which he spent with his relative aboard, and thus dropped in for the whole performance. He had been employed in helping to spot, and had lived up a mast till the ship sank, when he stepped off into the water and swam about till he was fished out and put ashore. By that time, the tale goes, his engine-room-dried khaki had shrunk half-way up his legs and arms, in which costume he reported himself to the War Office, and pleaded for one little day's extension of leave to make himself decent. 'Not a bit of it,' said the War Office. 'If you choose to spend your leave playing with sailor men and getting wet all over, that's *your* concern. You will return to duty by to-night's boat.' (This may be a libel on the W.O., but it sounds very like them.) 'And he had to,' said the boy, 'but I expect he spent the next week at Headquarters telling fat generals all about the fight.'

'And, of course, the Admiralty gave *you* all lots of leave?'

'Us? Yes, heaps. We had nothing to do except clean down and oil up, and be ready to go to sea again in a few hours.'

That little fact was brought out at the end of almost every destroyer's report. 'Having returned to base at such and such a time, I took in oil, etc., and reported ready for sea at ---- o'clock.' When you think of the amount of work a ship needs even after peace manoeuvres, you can realise what has to be done on the heels of an action. And, as there is nothing like housework for the troubled soul of a woman, so a general clean-up is good for sailors. I had this from a petty officer who had also passed through deep waters. 'If you've seen your best friend go from alongside you, and your own officer, and your own boat's crew with him, and things of that kind, a man's best comfort is small variegated jobs which he is damned for continuous.'

The Silent Navy

Presently my friend of the destroyer went back to his stark, desolate life, where feelings do not count, and the fact of his being cold, wet, sea-sick, sleepless, or dog-tired had no bearing whatever on his business, which was to turn out at any hour in any weather and do or endure, decently, according to ritual, what that hour and that weather demanded. It is hard to reach the kernel of Navy minds. The unbribable seas and mechanisms they work on and through have given them the simplicity of elements and machines. The habit of dealing with swift accident, a life of closest and strictest association with their own caste as well as contact with all kinds of men all earth over, have added an immense cunning to those qualities; and that they are from early youth cut out of all feelings that may come between them and their ends, makes them more incomprehensible than Jesuits, even to their own people. What, then, must they be to the enemy?

Here is a Service which prowls forth and achieves, at the lowest, something of a victory. How far-reaching a one only the war's end will reveal. It returns in gloomy silence, broken by the occasional hoot of the long-shore loafer, after issuing a bulletin which though it may enlighten the professional mind does not exhilarate the layman. Meantime the enemy triumphs, wirelessly, far and wide. A few frigid and perfunctory-seeming contradictions are put forward against his resounding claims; a Naval expert or two is heard talking 'off'; the rest is silence. Anon, the enemy, after a prodigious amount of explanation which not even the neutrals seem to take any interest in, revises his claims, and, very modestly, enlarges his losses. Still no sign. After weeks there appears a document giving our version of the affair, which is as colourless, detached, and scrupulously impartial as the findings of a prize-court. It opines that the list of enemy losses which it submits 'give the minimum in regard to numbers though it is possibly not entirely accurate in regard to the particular class of vessel, especially those that were sunk during the night attacks.' Here the matter rests and remains – just like our blockade. There is an insolence about it all that makes one gasp.

Yet that insolence springs naturally and unconsciously as an oath, out of the same spirit that caused the destroyer to pick up the dog. The reports themselves, and tenfold more the stories not in the reports, are charged with it, but no words by any outsider can reproduce just that professional tone and touch. A man writing home after the fight, points out that the great consolation for not having cleaned up the enemy altogether was that 'anyhow those East Coast devils' – a fellow-squadron, if you please, which up till Jutland had had most of the fighting – 'were not there. They missed that show. We were as cock-ahoop as a girl who had been to a dance that her sister has missed.'

This was one of the figures in that dance:

'A little British destroyer, her midships rent by a great shell meant for a battle-cruiser; exuding steam from every pore; able to go ahead but not to steer; unable to get out of anybody's way, likely to be rammed by any one of a dozen ships; her syren whimpering: 'Let me through! Make way!'; her crew fallen in aft, dressed in life-belts ready for her final plunge, and cheering wildly as it might have been an enthusiastic crowd when the King passes.'

Let us close on that note. We have been compassed about so long and so blindingly by wonders and miracles; so overwhelmed by revelations of the spirit of men in the basest and most high; that we have neither time to keep tally of these furious days, nor mind to discern upon which hour of them our world's fate hung.

THE NEUTRAL

Brethren, how shall it fare with me
  When the war is laid aside,
If it be proven that I am he
  For whom a world has died?

If it be proven that all my good,
  And the greater good I will make,
Were purchased me by a multitude
  Who suffered for my sake?

That I was delivered by mere mankind
  Vowed to one sacrifice,
And not, as I hold them, battle-blind,
  But dying with opened eyes?

That they did not ask me to draw the sword
  When they stood to endure their lot,
What they only looked to me for a word,

And I answered I knew them not?
If it be found, when the battle clears,
Their death has set me free,
Then how shall I live with myself through
the years
Which they have bought for me?

Brethren, how must it fare with me,
Or how am I justified,
If it be proven that I am he
For whom mankind has died;
If it be proven that I am he
Who being questioned denied?